我的名著美文

人不是生来就要被打败的

英汉对照　词汇解析　语法讲解　励志语录

张晓坤　编著

中国纺织出版社

图书在版编目（CIP）数据

我的名著美文：人不是生来就要被打败的：英文 / 张晓坤编著 . -- 北京：中国纺织出版社，2019.4
　ISBN 978-7-5180-5091-8

Ⅰ . ①我… Ⅱ . ①张… Ⅲ . ①英语－语言读物②世界文学－作品综合集 Ⅳ . ① H319.4：Ⅰ

中国版本图书馆 CIP 数据核字（2018）第 116711 号

责任编辑：武洋洋　　责任校对：武风余　　责任印制：储志伟

中国纺织出版社出版发行
地址：北京市朝阳区百子湾东里A407号楼　邮政编码：100124
销售电话：010—67004422　传真：010—87155801
http://www.c-textilep.com
E-mail:faxing@c-textilep.com
中国纺织出版社天猫旗舰店
官方微博http://www.weibo.com/2119887771
三河市延风印装有限公司印刷　各地新华书店经销
2019年4月第1版第1次印刷
开本：880×1230　1/32　印张：6.5
字数：210千字　定价：39.80元

凡购本书，如有缺页、倒页、脱页，由本社图书营销中心调换

前言

　　思想结晶改变人生命运，经典美文提高生活品位。曾几何时，一个字，触动你的心弦；一句话，让你泪流满面；一篇短文，让你重拾信心，勇敢面对生活给你的考验。这就是语言的魅力。通过阅读优美的英文短文，不仅能够扩大词汇量，掌握单词的用法，了解语法，学习地道的表达，更让你的心灵如沐春风，得到爱的呵护和情感的滋养。

　　岁月流转，经典永存。针对英语学习爱好者的需要，编者精心选取了难易适中的英语经典美文，为你提供一场丰富多彩的文学盛宴。本书采用中英文对照的形式，便于读者理解。每篇美文后都附有单词解析、语法知识点、经典名句三大版块，让你在欣赏完一篇美文后，还能扩充词汇量、巩固语法知识、斟酌文中好句，并感悟人生。在一篇篇不同题材风格的英语美文中，你总能找到引起你心灵共鸣的一篇。

　　读一本新书恰似坠入爱河，是场冒险。你得全身心地投入进去。翻开书页之时，从前言直至封底你或许都知之甚少。但谁又不是呢？字里行间的只言片语不总是正确的。

　　有时候你会发现，人们自我推销时是一种形象，等你在深入了解后，他们就完全变样了。有时故事的叙述流于表面，朴实的语言，平淡的情节，但阅读过半后，你却发觉这本书真是出乎意料的妙不可言，而这种感受只能靠自己去感悟！

阅读之乐，腹有诗书气自华；阅读之美，活水云影共天光。阅读可以放逐百年孤独，阅读可以触摸千年月光。阅读中有眼前的收获，阅读中也有诗和远方。

让我们静下心来感受英语美文的温度，在英语美文中仔细品味似曾相识的细腻情感，感悟生命和人性的力量。

编者
2018年6月

目录

01 Old Man and Sea
　老人与海 ··· 001

02 1984
　一九八四 ··· 005

03 A Farewell to Arms
　永别了，武器 ··· 010

04 A Little Princess
　小公主 ··· 014

05 Adam Bede
　亚当·比德 ··· 019

06 Alice in Wonderland
　爱丽丝梦游仙境 ··· 023

07 Araby
　阿拉比 ··· 027

08 Clarissa
　克拉丽莎 ··· 031

09 Common Sense
　常识 ··· 035

10 Death of a Salesman
　推销员之死 ··· 040

11 Emma
　爱玛 ··· 044

12 For Whom the Bell Tolls
　丧钟为谁而鸣 ··· 049

13 Gone with the Wind
飘 ··· 053

14 Great Expectations
远大前程 ··· 058

15 Hard Times
艰难时世 ··· 062

16 Ivanhoe
艾凡赫 ··· 066

17 Jane Eyre
简·爱 ··· 071

18 Jude the Obscure
无名的裘德 ··· 076

19 Love of Life
热爱生命 ··· 080

20 Lucky Jim
幸运的吉姆 ··· 084

21 Mansfield Park
曼斯菲尔德庄园 ····································· 089

22 Mrs. Dalloway
达洛维夫人 ··· 094

23 Oliver Twist
雾都孤儿 ··· 099

24 On Love
论爱情 ··· 105

25 Pamela
帕米拉 ··· 110

26 Pride and Prejudice
傲慢与偏见 ··· 114

27 Sense and Sensibility
理智与情感 ··· 119

Contents 目录

28 Sister Carrie
嘉莉妹妹 ··· 124

29 Tender is the Night
夜色温柔 ··· 129

30 Tess of the D'Urbervilles
德伯家的苔丝 ·· 134

31 The Adventures of Huckleberry Finn
哈克贝利·费恩历险记 ·· 139

32 The Adventures of Tom Sawyer
汤姆·索亚历险记 ··· 144

33 The Call of Nature
野性的呼唤 ··· 149

34 The Catcher in the Rye
麦田里的守望者 ··· 153

35 The French Lieutenant's Women
法国中尉的女人 ··· 157

36 The Gift of the Magi
麦琪的礼物 ··· 162

37 The Grapes of Wrath
愤怒的葡萄 ··· 166

38 The Great Gatsby
了不起的盖茨比 ··· 172

39 The Lord of the Flies
蝇王 ·· 176

40 The Merchant of Venice
威尼斯商人 ··· 181

41 The Plain Man and His Wife
平凡人和他的妻子 ··· 187

42 The Rainbow
彩虹 ·· 192

43 The Scarlet Letter

红字 ·· 197

01 Old Man and Sea
老人与海

The shark **swung** over and the old man saw his eye was not alive and then he swung over once again, wrapping himself in two loops of the rope. The old man knew that he was dead but the shark would not accept it. Then, on his back, with his tail **lashing** and his **jaws** clicking, the shark **plowed** over the water as a speed-boat does. The water was white where his tail beat it and three-quarters of his body was clear above the water when the rope came **taut**, shivered, and then **snapped**. The shark lay quietly for a little while on the surface and the old man watched him. Then he went down very slowly.

"He took about forty pounds," the old man said aloud. He took my **harpoon** too and all the rope, he thought, and now my fish bleeds again and there will be others.

He did not like to look at the fish anymore since he had been **mutilated**. When the fish had been hit it was as though he himself were hit.

But I killed the shark that hit my fish, he thought. And he was the biggest dentuso that I have ever seen. And God knows that I have seen big ones.

鲨鱼翻了个身，老人发现他的眼睛已无生气；接着它又翻了个身，这样一来它把自己缠了两圈绳子。老人知道这鲨鱼快死了，但它还是不肯认输。接下来，它肚皮朝上，尾巴扑打着海面、双颚嘎吱作响，像一条快艇般在水面上划出一道痕迹。它的尾巴把水拍打得泛出白色，四分之三的身体露出水面，这时绳子绷得很紧，颤抖着，最后啪的一声断了。老人盯着鲨鱼，它在水面上静静地躺了片刻，然后慢慢地沉了下去。

"它扯去了大约四十磅肉，"老人大声地说着，"它还带走了我的鱼叉及所有的绳子"，他心想，"而且现在我这条鱼又在流血，还会来其他鲨鱼的。"

他不想再看一眼这条鱼，因为它已经残缺不全了。鱼遭到袭击的时候，他感到就像自己受到袭击一样。

但是，袭击鱼的鲨鱼被我杀死了，他这样想着。它是我见过的最大的灰鲭鲨。上天作证，我也见过一些大的。

我的名著美文：人不是生来就要被打败的

It was too good to last, he thought. I wish it had been a dream now and that I had never **hooked** the fish and was alone in bed on the newspapers.

"But man is not made for defeat," he said. "A man can be destroyed but not defeated." I am sorry that I killed the fish though, he thought. Now the bad time is coming and I do not even have the harpoon. The dentuso is cruel and able and strong and intelligent. But I was more intelligent than he was. Perhaps not, he thought. Perhaps I was only better armed.

注释：dentuso 西班牙语，意为"锋利的"，是当地对灰鲭鲨的俗称。

美好的事物持续的时间都不长，他想着。现在，我只希望这是一场梦，我根本没有钓到这条鱼，而是正独自躺在铺着旧报纸的床上。

"但人不是生来就要被打败的，"他说道，"人可以被摧毁，但不可以被击败。" "虽然我很抱歉杀了这条大鱼。"他这样想着。他想：现在糟糕的时刻要到了，我甚至连鱼叉也没有。灰鲭鲨残忍、能干、强壮又聪明。但是我比它更聪明，或许并没有。他想，也许只是我的武器比较好。

单词解析 Word Analysis

swing [swiŋ] v. 突然转向

例 He swung the camera around to face the opposite direction.
他突然将相机调至反方向。

lash [læʃ] v. 鞭打，猛打

例 Huge waves lashed the shore.
巨浪拍打着海岸。

jaw [dʒɔ:] n. 下巴，颌

例 The punch broke my jaw.
这一拳打坏了我的下巴。

plow [plau] v. 耕地；费力穿过

例 Who will milk the cow and plow the land?
谁能挤牛奶并耕田呀？

taut [tɔːt] *adj.* 紧的，绷紧的

例 The skin of the drum is taut.
鼓面很紧。

snap [snæp] *v.* （咔嚓）断掉，断裂

例 The wind snapped the tree in two.
风把树折成了两段。

harpoon [haːpuːn] *n.* 鱼叉

例 The harpoon drove deep into the body of the whale.
鱼叉深深地刺进鲸的体内。

mutilate ['mjuːtileit] *v.* 使残废，使残缺不全；严重损坏

例 Intruders slashed and mutilated some paintings.
有人闯进来，破坏了几幅油画。

hook [huk] *v.* 钩住，钓住

例 It was the biggest sardine I ever hooked.
那是我钓到的最大一条沙丁鱼。

语法知识点 Grammar Points

① **Then, on his back, with his tail lashing and his jaws clicking, the shark plowed over the water as a speed-boat does.**

"With his tail lashing and his jaws clicking" 作伴随状语，表状态，相当于"那时，它的尾巴击打着海面，它的双颚嘎吱作响"。整句话的主语是"the shark"，谓语动词为"plowed"。

相似用法：He felt more uneasy with the whole class staring at him.
在全班同学的注视下，他感到更加不自然。
在上面的例句中，主语是"he"，谓语动词为"felt"。

"plow"本意是耕种，耕田。在这里涉及了一个修辞手法：隐喻。暗指鲨鱼划过海面的痕迹就像耕地的痕迹一样。这样的描写更加生动形象。

相似用法如："Snow clothes the ground."，地上覆盖了薄薄的一层雪。

② **I wish it had been a dream now and that I had never hooked the fish and was alone in bed on the newspapers.**

本句中涉及了wish引导的虚拟语气：主语+wish (that) +从句主语+would/could have或had+过去分词，用于对过去的事情表示遗憾或后悔。

③ **"But man is not made for defeat", he said. "A man can be destroyed but not defeated."**

be made for "最理想的，最适合的"。如："Allowance should be made for the difficulties of his problems." 应当体谅他的艰难处境。

经典名句 Famous Classics

1. A child is better unborn than untaught.
   养不教，父之过。

2. None is so old that he hopes not for years of life.
   人活百岁不嫌长。

3. Practice makes perfect.
   熟能生巧。

4. Poverty is the mother of all arts.
   贫穷是一切艺术之母。

5. Nothing is ever done in a hurry.
   匆匆忙忙办不成任何事。

6. Practice is better than precept.
   身教胜于言教。

7. Nothing stake, nothing draw.
   不入虎穴焉得虎子。

8. A clear conscience is a sure card.
   光明磊落，胜券在握。

02 1984 一九八四

His eyes re-focused on the page. He discovered that while he sat helplessly **musing** he had also been writing, as though by automatic action. And it was no longer the same cramped, awkward handwriting as before. His pen had slid voluptuously over the smooth paper, printing in large neat capitals

DOWN WITH BIG BROTHER
DOWN WITH BIG BROTHER
DOWN WITH BIG BROTHER
DOWN WITH BIG BROTHER
DOWN WITH BIG BROTHER

over and over again, filling half a page.

He could not help feeling a twinge of panic. It was absurd, since the writing of those particular words was not more dangerous than the initial act of opening the diary, but for a moment he was tempted to tear out the spoiled pages and abandon the **enterprise** altogether.

He did not do so, however, because he knew that it was useless. Whether he wrote DOWN WITH BIG BROTHER, or whether he refrained from writing it, made no difference. Whether he went on with the diary, or whether he did not go on

他的目光又回到纸面上。他发现，当他无助地沉思时，他也一直在写东西，好像是不由自主地在写一样。字迹也不似从前那般又小又密、难以辨认了。他的笔在光滑的纸上流畅地写着整齐的字，字母全为大写——

打倒老大哥
打倒老大哥
打倒老大哥
打倒老大哥
打倒老大哥

这样一遍又一遍地写着，写满了半张纸。

他不禁感到一阵恐慌。这是荒谬的，因为写下这些特定的词并不比开始写日记这一行为更危险，但是有那么一会儿，他真想撕毁损坏的那几页，连同计划也一起放弃。

不过，他并没有这样做，因为他知道就算这样做了也没用。无论写下"打倒老大哥"，还是忍住不写，二者没有什么不同。无论他是否继续写日记，也没有什么不同。思想警察一样会找到他的。他已经犯

with it, made no difference. The Thought Police would get him just the same. He had committed — would still have committed, even if he had never set pen to paper — the essential crime that contained all others in itself. Thoughtcrime, they called it. Thoughtcrime was not a thing that could be concealed for ever. You might **dodge** successfully for a while, even for years, but sooner or later they were bound to get you.

It was always at night — the arrests invariably happened at night. The sudden jerk out of sleep, the rough hand shaking your shoulder, the lights glaring in your eyes, the ring of hard faces round the bed. In the vast majority of cases there was no trial, no report of the arrest. People simply disappeared, always during the night. Your name was removed from the registers, every record of everything you had ever done was wiped out, your one-time existence was denied and then forgotten. You were abolished, **annihilated**: **vaporized** was the usual word.

下了——即使他从来没有在纸上落笔，也是犯下了——包含其他所有罪行的根本大罪。人们称之为"思想罪"。思想罪是不可以永远隐藏的。你可能短暂地藏匿一阵，甚至几年，但迟早他们会逮到你。

一直是在夜里——逮捕总是在晚上发生。突然从睡梦中惊醒，一双粗鲁的手在摇晃你的肩膀，炫目的灯光射进你的眼里，床边围了一圈严酷的脸。在绝大多数情况下，没有审判，没有逮捕的报告。人们就这样消失了，而且总是在夜里消失。你登记册上的名字会除掉，你所做过的所有事情的每一个记录都会被抹去，你的存在被否认，然后被遗忘。你被铲除了，被消灭了："蒸发"是常用的词汇。

单词解析 *Word Analysis*

muse [mjuːz] 沉思，冥想

例 I sat quietly, musing on the events of the day.
我静静地坐着，沉思着一天中发生的事。

enterprise ['entəpraiz] n. 计划；事业

例 It seemed to be an ill-judged enterprise.
这似乎是一项不明智的计划。

dodge [dɔdʒ] v. 躲闪；回避

例 The girl dodged behind a tree to hide from the other children.
这女孩躲在树后不让其他小孩发现。

annihilate [ə'naiəleit] v. 歼灭；毁灭

例 The human race has enough weapons to annihilate itself.
人类有足以消灭自己的武器。

vaporize ['veipəraiz] v. 蒸发；（使）汽化

例 You can vaporize it and then condense it back again.
你可以先把它汽化，然后再将它冷凝。

语法知识点 *Grammar Points*

① He discovered that while he sat helplessly musing he had also been writing, as though by automatic action.

整句话为由that引导的宾语从句，从句中又涉及while引导的时间状语从句，表示"当……"。

"as though" 好像，仿佛

例 It looked as though it might rain at any minute.
看上去好像随时都会下雨。

② He could not help feeling a twinge of panic.

"can/could not help +doing" 不禁……，忍不住……

例 She could not help crying at the sight of her mother.
她一看到妈妈就忍不住哭了出来。

"a twinge of" 一阵思绪（通常为不愉快的），文学用法。

例 I felt a twinge of envy for the people who lived there.
我对住在那儿的人产生了一阵妒忌。

③ **Whether he wrote DOWN WITH BIG BROTHER, or whether he refrained from writing it, made no difference.**

"refrain from +doing/n." 忍住；抑制

例 I made a terrific effort to refrain from tears.
我强制忍住眼泪。

④ **You might dodge successfully for a while, even for years, but sooner or later they were bound to get you.**

"be bound to" 一定……，注定……

例 Your education is bound to shape your world view.
一个人的教育决定着他的世界观。

经典名句 Famous Classics

1. A common danger causes common action.
   同仇敌忾。

2. Put another man's child in your bosom, and he will creep at your elbow.
   别人的孩子养不亲。

3. A contented mind is perpetual feast.
   知足常乐。

4. Money is wise, it knows its way.
   金钱聪明，知道路径。

5. One of the best ways to keep friendship is to return it.
   要保持友谊，须报之以友谊。

6. Money is the sinews of war.
   金钱是战争的命脉。

7. People who live in glass houses have no right to throw stones.
   正人先正己。

8. One rotten apple spoils the whole barrel.
   一粒老鼠屎坏了一锅粥。

9. Pigs love that lie together.
猪躺在一起不嫌脏。（小人凑在一起臭味相投。）

读书笔记

03 A Farewell to Arms
永别了，武器

The night at the hotel, in our room with the long empty hall outside and our shoes outside the door, a thick **carpet** on the floor of the room, outside the windows the rain falling and in the room light and pleasant and cheerful, then the light out and it exciting with **smooth** sheets and the bed comfortable, feeling that we had come home, feeling no longer alone, waking in the night to find the other one there, and not gone away; all other things were unreal. We slept when we were tired and if we woke the other one woke too so one was not alone. Often a man wishes to be alone and a girl wishes to be alone too and if they love each other they are **jealous** of that in each other, but I can truly say we never felt that. We could feel alone when we were together, alone against the others. It has only happened to me like that once. I have been alone while I was with many girls and that is the way that you can be most lonely. But we were never lonely and never afraid when we were together. I know that the night is not the same as the day: that all things are different, that the things of

住在旅店的那晚，我们的鞋子摆放在门外，房门连着一个空荡的长廊，屋内铺着厚厚的地毯，窗外的雨一直在下。屋内光线充足，我们感到心满意足，灯光熄灭后，光滑的被单和舒适的床让我们激动不已，仿佛回到家了一样。不再感到孤单，夜里醒来发现爱人没有离开，依然在身边，这一切都好得不真实。我们感觉倦了就睡，如果一方醒来，另一方也会跟着醒来，所以没有人感到孤独。通常不管男人还是女人都会想独处一会儿，如果他们彼此相爱就会嫉妒对方的独处。但我敢肯定我们从未有这种感觉。我们在一起时也会感到孤独，这种孤单与他人格格不入。我目前为止只有过一次这样的经历。和许多女孩待在一起的时候我觉得孤独，其实这是最让人孤独的时刻。但当我们（我和凯瑟琳）在一起时，我从未感到孤独，也从未有过恐惧感。我知道白天和夜晚是不同的：所有的一切都不同；白天无法解释夜晚的事情，因为夜晚的事

A Farewell to Arms 永别了，武器

the night cannot be explained in the day, because they do not then exist, and the night can be a **dreadful** time for lonely people once their loneliness has started. But with Catherine there was almost no difference in the night except that it was an even better time. If people bring so much courage to this world the world has to kill them to break them, so of course it kills them. The world breaks every one and afterward many are strong at the broken places. But those that will not break it kills. It kills the very good and the very gentle and the very brave **impartially**. If you are none of these you can be sure it will kill you too but there will be no special hurry.

情在白天根本不存在；一旦触发了孤独感，夜晚会使孤独的人恐惧。但和凯瑟琳在一起，白天和夜晚没什么分别，除了夜晚甚至比白天更好。如果一个人是带着勇气来到这个世界的，为了将他们击倒，这个世界只能摧残他们，当然了，最后会把他们都杀掉。因此，世界摧残所有人，后来人们会在受打击的地方看起来很坚强。但对于无法击倒的人，世界会迫害他们。世界会"一视同仁"地残害特别善良的人，特别温柔的人以及特别勇敢的人。如果你不是这些人中的任何一种，世界也同样会杀死你，只是并不是那么着急罢了。

单词解析 Word Analysis

carpet ['kɑːpɪt] *n.* 地毯，绒毯

例 The carpet was a wedding present from the Prime Minister.
这张地毯是首相送的结婚礼物。

smooth [smuːð] *adj.* 光滑的；流畅的；柔软的

例 Over the years, the stone steps had worn smooth.
日久天长，石阶已经磨得光溜溜的。

jealous ['dʒeləs] *adj.* 妒忌的；羡慕的

be jealous of 嫉妒……

例 She's jealous of my success.
她忌妒我的成功。

011

我的名著美文：人不是生来就要被打败的

dreadful ['dredfl] *adj.* 可怕的；令人畏惧的

例 They suffered dreadful injuries.
他们严重受伤。

impartially [,ɪmˈpɑːʃəlɪ] *adv.* 公平地，无私地

例 He has vowed to oversee the elections impartially.
他已宣誓公平公正地监督竞选。

语法知识点 Grammar Points

① **We slept when we were tired and if we woke the other one woke too so one was not alone.**

"so one was not alone" 的正常语序为 "so no one was alone"，没人感到孤单。

② **Often a man wishes to be alone and a girl wishes to be alone too and if they love each other they are jealous of that in each other, but I can truly say we never felt that.**

"if" 引导条件句，that指代wish to be alone。
"say" 后面省略了that，接宾语从句。

③ **I know that the night is not the same as the day: that all things are different, that the things of the night cannot be explained in the day, because they do not then exist, and the night can be a dreadful time for lonely people once their loneliness has started.**

"the same as" 与……同样的，和……一样

例 Driving a boat is not the same as driving a car.
驾船和开车不是一回事。

"that all things are different, that the things of the night cannot be explained in the day" 中的两个that引导主语从句。

"once" 引导条件状语从句，一旦……

例 Once wholesale prices are deregulated, consumer prices will also rise.
一旦批发价格放开，零售价格也会随之上涨。

012

A Farewell to Arms
永别了，武器

经典名句 Famous Classics

1. Money is often lost for want of money.
   往往由于缺乏金钱而丧失金钱。

2. Trust the ear less than the eye.
   宁可相信眼睛，勿要相信耳朵。（眼见为实，耳听为虚。）

3. None knows the weight of another's burden.
   看人挑担不吃力。

4. Money is round, and rolls away.
   圆圆钱币，滚走容易。

5. Money isn't everything.
   金钱并非是万能的。

6. A good beginning makes a good ending.
   善始者必善终。

7. Never trust another what you should do yourself.
   自己该做的事，绝不要委托别人代做。

8. No man knows when he shall die, although he knows he must die.
   纵然知其难免一死，人却难料何时身亡。

9. A belly full of gluttony will never study willingly.
   追求吃喝的人绝不会自觉学习。

读书笔记

A Little Princess
小公主

Once on a dark winter's day, when the yellow fog hung so thick and heavy in the streets of London that the lamps were lighted and the shop windows **blazed** with gas as they do at night, an odd-looking little girl sat in a cab with her father and was driven rather slowly through the big **thoroughfares**.

She sat with her feet **tucked** under her, and **leaned** against her father, who held her in his arms, as she stared out of the window at the passing people with a **queer** old-fashioned thoughtfulness in her big eyes.

She was such a little girl that one did not expect to see such a look on her small face. It would have been an old look for a child of twelve, and Sara Crewe was only seven. The fact was, however, that she was always dreaming and thinking odd things and could not herself remember any time when she had not been thinking things about grown-up people and the world they belonged to. She felt as if she had lived a long, long time.

...

It seemed to her many years since

在一个冬天的夜里，昏黄的浓雾笼罩在亮着街灯的伦敦大街上，油灯照例将商店的橱窗照得通明。一个相貌奇特的小女孩和她的父亲坐在计程车里，缓慢地在街上行进。

她蜷起双腿，倚靠在父亲的臂弯里。她呆呆地望向窗外匆匆而过的人流，从她大大的眼睛里透露着一种老式的，又若有所思的神色。

没人想到从这么一张小脸上看到如此成熟的表情。这种神情即便出现在一个十二岁的孩子脸上都显得老气横秋，而萨拉·克鲁才只有七岁。可实际上，她经常会幻想或想起一些奇怪的事情，连她自己都不记得她有哪一刻没有在想成年人的事情和属于他们的世界。她觉得自己似乎活了很长的时间，很长的时间。

……

对她来说，她已经为"那个地方"（她经常这样称呼它）做了好几年的思想工作了。她一生下来，她的母亲就去世了，因此她从来都不认识

he had begun to prepare her mind for "the place", as she always called it. Her mother had died when she was born, so she had never known or missed her. Her young, handsome, rich, petting father seemed to be the only relation she had in the world. They had always played together and been fond of each other. She only knew he was rich because she had heard people say so when they thought she was not listening, and she had also heard them say that when she grew up she would be rich, too. She did not know all that being rich meant. She had always lived in a beautiful **bungalow**, and had been used to seeing many servants who made salaams to her and called her "Missee **Sahib**," and gave her her own way in everything. She had had toys and pets and an **ayah** who worshipped her, and she had gradually learned that people who were rich had these things. That, however, was all she knew about it.

母亲也并不会思念她。似乎她和这个世界唯一的联系就是她那年轻、帅气、富有又十分宠爱她的父亲。他们总是一起玩耍，相亲相爱。她仅仅只是知道她父亲很有钱，这是人们背地里说的，但是她都听见了；她还听到人们说她长大了也会很有钱。她不知道有钱到底意味着什么。她过去一直住在漂亮的公寓里，有很多仆人给她问安，称呼她"Missee Sahib"，让她什么都随心所欲。她有很多玩具、宠物，还有个极度疼爱她的奶妈，她慢慢知道了这些东西只有有钱人才能拥有。然而，这些就是她能理解到的所有了。

单词解析 Word Analysis

blaze [bleiz] *v.* 发光，照耀

例 The sun blazed down from a clear blue sky.
耀眼的阳光从清澈蔚蓝的天空中照射下来。

thoroughfare [ˈθʌrəfeə] *n.* 大道，大街

例 Don't park your car on a busy thoroughfare.
别把车停在繁忙的大街上。

015

tuck [tʌk] v. 折叠，卷起
例 The sheets should be tucked in neatly.
床单的四边应该整整齐齐地折好。

lean [liːn] v. (使)倚靠，斜靠
例 She leaned her bike against the wall.
她把自行车靠在了这面墙上。

queer [kwɪə(r)] adj. 奇怪的
例 His face was a queer pink color.
他的脸粉得奇怪。

bungalow [ˈbʌŋɡələʊ] n. [英]平房；[美]单层小屋
例 A door opened in a bungalow across the avenue.
街对面的那座房子的门打开了。

sahib [saːb] n. (印度旧时对欧洲男子的尊称)先生，老爷
例 "It is most urgent, sahib," he said.
"事情非常紧急，先生。"他说。

ayah [ˈaɪə] n. 女仆，奶妈
例 Mary had been raised by her Ayah.
玛丽一直是由她的奶妈抚养长大的。

语法知识点 Grammar Points

① **She sat with her feet tucked under her, and leaned against her father, who held her in his arms, as she stared out of the window at the passing people with a queer old-fashioned thoughtfulness in her big eyes.**

整句话的主语是"she"，两个动词"sat"和"leaned"由连词"and"连接。"who"引导非限制性定语从句，指代"her father"。"as"做连词，"当……的时候"，引导时间状语从句。

A Little Princess
小公主 04

② **She was such a little girl that one did not expect to see such a look on her small face. It would have been an old look for a child of twelve, and Sara Crewe was only seven.**

"such...that" 如此……以至于

例 The boy ran so fast that I couldn't catch him.
那个男孩跑得太快了，以至于我抓不住他。

"would have done" 为虚拟语气，与过去事实相反（整篇小说的时态为一般过去时，因此用与过去事实相反的虚拟语气）。

例 We would have held the story over until the next day.
我们原本想把报道推迟到第二天的。

③ **The fact was, however, that she was always dreaming and thinking odd things and could not herself remember any time when she had not been thinking things about grown-up people and the world they belonged to.**

此句中用双重否定"not... not"（即：否定+否定）来强调肯定，表示小女孩无时无刻不在思考一些奇怪的事情。

例 He was nothing if not clever.
他很聪明。

④ **She had always lived in a beautiful bungalow, and had been used to seeing many servants who made salaams to her and called her "Missee Sahib," and gave her her own way in everything.**

"be used to doing" 习惯于做……

例 I wasn't used to doing things by myself.
我不习惯独自做事情。

"give sb. sth." 或 "give sth. to sb." 都表示给某人某物。"gave her her own way" 中，断句情况如下：gave her/ her own way，第一个her作直接宾语，her own way作为一个整体，作间接宾语。

经典名句 Famous Classics

1. Trust not a new friend, nor an old enemy.
   新友不可信，宿敌需提防。

017

我的名著美文：人不是生来就要被打败的

2. Pigs may fly, but they are very unlikely birds.
   猪儿纵会飞，终究不是鸟。

3. A good name is better than gold.
   美名胜金玉。

4. Trust yourself only, and another shall not betray you.
   唯有相信自己，他人才不背叛你。

5. A friend is a second self.
   朋友是第二个自我。

6. Night is the mother of counsel.
   夜晚孕育深思熟虑。

7. Truth fears no colours.
   真理是驳不倒的。

8. A good beginning is half done.
   良好的开始是成功的一半。

读书笔记

05 Adam Bede
亚当·比德

Mr. Casson's person was by no means of that common type which can be allowed to pass without description. On a front view it appeared to consist principally of two spheres, bearing about the same relation to each other as the earth and the moon: that is to say, the lower sphere might be said, at a rough guess, to be thirteen times larger than the upper which naturally performed the function of a mere satellite and **tributary**. But here the resemblance ceased, for Mr. Casson's head was not at all a **melancholy**-looking satellite nor was it a "spotty globe", as Milton has irreverently called the moon; on the contrary, no head and face could look more **sleek** and healthy, and its expression—which was chiefly confined to a pair of round and **ruddy** cheeks, the slight knot and interruptions forming the nose and eyes being scarcely worth mention—was one of jolly contentment, only tempered by that sense of personal **dignity** which usually made itself felt in his attitude and bearing. This sense of dignity could hardly be considered excessive in a man who had been

卡森先生长得很是不一般，旁人定会对其长相加以评论。从正面看，他的身体主要由两个球体组成，它们与地球和月球的关系相似：也就是说，粗略估计，下面的球比上面的大十三倍。而上面的球，是卫星或者只是附属。相似之处仅此而已。因为卡森的头并不像一个忧郁的卫星，也不像一个"斑点的地球"——米尔顿这样不敬地称呼月球。相反，没有人的头部和脸部看起来更光滑健康了，对于其面部——主要局限于圆润红润的脸颊，尽管他的鼻子像肉团，眼睛眯成了一条缝，一副心满意足的表情。只有在举手投足间摆点架子才能体现尊严感。有这种想法一点也不过分，因为他已经在名门望族当了15年的差，而且现如今身处高位，与地位低于他的人相处摆点架子是很有必要的。如何放下架子走向职场菜鸟来满足他的好奇心，这个问题在过去的五分钟内一直在卡森的脑海中盘旋。最后，他拿定了主意，

019

butler to "the family" for fifteen years, and who, in his present high position, was necessarily very much in contact with his inferiors. How to reconcile his dignity with the satisfaction of his curiosity by walking towards the Green was the problem that Mr. Casson had been revolving in his mind for the last five minutes; but when he had partly solved it by taking his hands out of his pockets, and thrusting them into the armholes of his waistcoat, by throwing his head on one side, and providing himself with an air of **contemptuous** indifference to whatever might fall under his notice, his thoughts were diverted by the approach of the horseman whom we lately saw pausing to have another look at our friend Adam, and who now pulled up at the door of the Donnithorne Arms.

把手从口袋里伸出来，又放到背心的袖孔里，头歪向一侧，好像在说，无论在他眼皮子底下发生什么他都不屑一顾。这时，他的思绪被越来越近的骑着马的人打断了，此人正是之前停下马打量亚当的那位老人。现在他停在了唐妮尚旅店的门口。

单词解析 Word Analysis

tributary [ˈtrɪbjətri] *n.* 附庸国；附属

例 England was his faithful tributary.
英格兰是他忠心的藩属。

melancholy [ˈmelənkəli] *adj.* 忧郁的

例 He fixed me with those luminous, empty eyes and his melancholy smile.
他忧郁地微笑着凝视着我，闪亮的眼睛里空无一物。

sleek [sliːk] *adj.* 时髦的；豪华的

例 She wore a sleek little black dress.

Adam Bede 亚当·比德

她穿了一条时髦的黑色连衣裙。

ruddy ['rʌdi] *adj.* 红润的，血色好的

例 He had a naturally ruddy complexion.
他的脸色天生红润。

dignity ['dɪɡnəti] *n.* 尊严；高尚；自豪；自尊

例 She's got too much dignity to descend to writing anonymous letter.
她是个自尊心很强的人，绝不会自贬身份去写匿名信。

contemptuous [kən'temptʃuəs] *adj.* 蔑视的，鄙视的

例 She gave a contemptuous little laugh.
她鄙夷地轻轻笑了笑。

语法知识点 *Grammar Points*

① **Mr. Casson's person was by no means of that common type which can be allowed to pass without description.**

"by no means of"决不、绝不会

例 This is by no means out of the ordinary.
这丝毫不足为奇。

② **...that is to say, the lower sphere might be said, at a rough guess, to be thirteen times larger than the upper which naturally performed the function of a mere satellite and tributary.**

"the upper"指代the upper sphere，后面的which引导限制性定语从句。
"that is to say"即"换句话说；更确切地说"的意思。

例 The English reader, that is to say, needs to make a double approach to American literature.
这就是说，英国读者看待美国文学，需要采取一种双重态度。

③ **How to reconcile his dignity with the satisfaction of his curiosity by walking towards the Green was the problem that Mr. Casson had been revolving in his mind for the last five minutes**

整个句子的主语为how引导的主语从句，how引导的主语从句例句如下：

> How he killed the man is still a mystery.
> 他是怎样杀害的那个男人仍旧是个谜。

"reconcile A with B" 协调A与B的关系

> It was hard to reconcile his career ambitions with the needs of his children.
> 他很难兼顾事业上的抱负和孩子们的需要。

经典名句 Famous Classics

1. Truth and love are two of the most powerful things in the world; and when they both go together they cannot easily be with-stood.
   真理和爱情是世界上力量最强大的两样东西，当它们两者走在一起时，它们是很难抵挡的。

2. Truth and roses have thorns about them.
   真理和玫瑰，身上皆有刺。

3. A life without a friend is like a life without a sun.
   人生没有朋友，犹如生活没有阳光。

4. A little is better than none.
   少胜于无。

5. Truth hath a good face, but ill clothes.
   真理面目和善，但衣衫褴褛。

6. Nightingales will not sing in a cage.
   夜莺困笼不唱歌。

7. Actions speak louder than words.
   行动胜过言语。

8. A man is never too old to learn.
   活到老，学到老。

9. You can't make bricks without straw.
   没有稻草，制砖难搞。（巧妇难为无米之炊。）

06 Alice in Wonderland
爱丽丝梦游仙境

But her sister sat still just as she left her, leaning her head on her hand, watching the setting sun, and thinking of little Alice and all her wonderful Adventures, till she too began dreaming after a fashion, and this was her dream:

First, she dreamed of little Alice herself, and once again the tiny hands were **clasped** upon her knee, and the bright eager eyes were looking up into hers——she could hear the very tones of her voice, and see that **queer** little toss of her head to keep back the wandering hair that would always get into her eyes——and still as she listened, or seemed to listen, the whole place around her became alive the strange creatures of her little sister's dream.

The long grass **rustled** at her feet as the White Rabbit hurried by—the frightened Mouse **splashed** his way through the neighbouring pool—she could hear the rattle of the teacups as the March Hare and his friends shared their never-ending meal, and the **shrill** voice of the Queen ordering off her unfortunate guests to execution——once more the pig-baby was sneezing on the Duchess's knee, while plates and

爱丽丝走后，她姐姐仍静静地坐在那里，用手撑着头，望着西下的夕阳，想起了小爱丽丝和她梦中的奇幻经历，就这样她自己也进入了梦乡。下面就是她的梦：

开始，她梦见了小爱丽丝本人，小爱丽丝又用双手抱住了膝盖，用明亮而热切的眼光望着她。她能听到小爱丽丝的声音，看到了小爱丽丝用略奇怪的方式摆了摆头，把蓬乱的头发捋顺了些，这是她常常见到的情景。当她听着爱丽丝讲述着梦中的那些奇异生物时，至少看起来是在听着，周围的环境开始变得富有生机。

白兔匆匆而过，弄得她脚下的草沙沙作响，受惊的老鼠在邻近的洞穴间窜来窜去。她还听到三月兔同它的朋友们共享着没完没了的美餐时茶杯碰撞得咯咯作响，以及王后命令处决她那不幸客人时的尖叫声。同时也听到猪宝宝在公爵夫人腿上打喷嚏的声音，以及盘碗的破碎声。甚至听到鹰头狮的尖叫声、壁虎写字时板岩石发出的吱吱声、被制裁的豚

dishes crashed around it—once more the shriek of the Gryphon, the squeaking of the Lizard's slate-pencil, and the choking of the suppressed guinea-pigs, filled the air, mixed up with the distant sobs of the miserable Mock Turtle.

So she sat on, with closed eyes, and half believed herself in Wonderland, though she knew she had but to open them again, and all would change to dull reality—the grass would be only rustling in the wind, and the pool **rippling** to the waving of the reeds—the rattling teacups would change to tinkling sheep-bells, and the Queen's shrill cries to the voice of the shepherd boy—and the sneeze of the baby, the shriek of the Gryphon, and all the other queer noises would change (she knew) to the confused **clamour** of the busy farm-yard—while the lowing of the cattle in the distance would take the place of the Mock Turtle's heavy sobs.

鼠的挣扎声等等。空气中充斥着这些声音，还混杂着远处传来的素甲鱼那哀戚的啜泣声。

于是她将身子坐正，闭着眼睛，不太确定自己真的到了奇幻世界。尽管她知道她只是重温旧梦，而一切终将回到现实：蒿草只是迎风作响，随风摆动的芦苇使池水泛起涟漪。茶杯的碰击声实际上是羊颈上的铃铛声，王后的尖叫也只是牧童的呵斥。猪宝宝的喷嚏声、鹰头狮的尖叫声和各种奇声怪音这一切都会变样（她原本就知道），这些只是乡村中繁忙季节的各种喧闹声。而在梦中变成素甲鱼的哀泣声的是远处耕牛的低吟。

单词解析 Word Analysis

clasp [klɑːsp] v 紧抱；扣住

例 He leaned forward, his hands clasped tightly together.
他俯身向前，双手紧握。

queer [kwɪə(r)] adj 古怪的；不适的

例 I could not help but think this is a very queer life.
我会忍不住觉得这是一种非常奇怪的生活。

Alice in Wonderland
爱丽丝梦游仙境 06

rustle ['rʌsl] *v.* 发出沙沙的声音
例 The leaves rustle in the wind.
树叶在风中沙沙作响。

splash [splæʃ] *v.* （使）溅起
例 Water splashed onto the floor.
水哗的一下溅到了地板上。

shrill [ʃril] *adj.* （声音）尖锐的，刺耳的；强烈的
例 The unearthly silence was broken by a shrill screaming.
一声尖叫打破了这可怕的寂静。

ripple ['ripl] *v.* （使）泛起涟漪
例 The sea rippled and sparkled.
海面波光粼粼。

clamour ['klæmə(r)] *n.* 喧闹声；嘈杂声；吵闹
例 The clamour for her resignation grew louder.
民众要求她辞职的呼声越来越高。

语法知识点 Grammar Points

① ...the frightened Mouse splashed his way through the neighbouring pool.

"splash one's way through" 从……中飞奔而过，从……中窜来窜去
例 He started to splash his way through the grass and mud.
他开始在草地和泥土间跳来跳去。

② ...she could hear the rattle of the teacups as the March Hare and his friends shared their never-ending meal, and the shrill voice of the Queen ordering off her unfortunate guests to execution.

"as" 引导时间状语从句，表示：当……
"order off" 勒令……退出比赛
例 His rudeness made the judge order him off immediately.
由于他的粗鲁，裁判让他立即退出比赛。

025

我的名著美文：人不是生来就要被打败的

③ ...once more the shriek of the Gryphon, the squeaking of the Lizard's slate-pencil, and the choking of the suppressed guinea-pigs, filled the air, mixed up with the distant sobs of the miserable Mock Turtle.

"mix up" 混杂，混在一起。在本句中为非谓语动词done的形式，表示被动，译为"被……混杂着"。

例 Don't mix up the two kinds of vegetable seeds.
别把两种蔬菜种子弄混了。

经典名句 Famous Classics

1. A wise man knows his own.
   智者有自知之明。

2. All beginnings are bad.
   万事开头难。

3. By falling we learn to go safely.
   吃一堑，长一智。

4. Truth has no need of rhetoric.
   真理无需华丽的辞藻。

5. An apple a day keeps the doctor away.
   一天一苹果，医生远离我。

6. Business is business.
   公事公办。

7. You can't make omelets without breaking eggs.
   不打破鸡蛋，就做不了蛋卷。（有失才有得。）

8. New brooms sweep clean.
   新官上任三把火。

9. Can the leopard change his spots?
   本性难移。

07 Araby
阿拉比

My uncle said he was very sorry he had forgotten. He said he believed in the old saying: "All work and no play makes Jack a dull boy." He asked me where I was going and, when I told him a second time, he asked did I know The Arab's Farewell to his Steed. When I left the kitchen he was about to recite the opening lines of the piece to my aunt.

I held a florin tightly in my hand as I **strode** down Buckingham Street towards the station. The sight of the streets **thronged** with buyers and glaring with gas recalled to me the purpose of my journey. I took my seat in a third-class carriage of a deserted train. After an intolerable delay the train moved out of the station slowly. It crept onward among ruinous houses and over the twinkling river. At Westland Row Station a crowd of people pressed to the carriage doors; but the porters moved them back, saying that it was a special train for the bazaar. I remained alone in the bare carriage. In a few minutes the train **drew up** beside an improvised wooden platform. I passed out on to the road and saw by the lighted dial of a

我的叔叔说他很抱歉他忘记了。他说他相信那句老话："总工作，不玩耍，人都会变傻。"他问我去哪里，当我又告诉他我要去哪儿时，他问我是否知道阿拉伯人怎样告别他的骏马。当我离开厨房时，他正准备向我的阿姨背诵开场白。

当我沿着白金汉大街走向车站时，我紧紧地握着一个弗罗林。看到街道上挤满了买家，汽油让街道发亮，我想起了此行的目的。我坐在一列空无一人的三等车厢里。经过让人无法忍受的延误，列车缓缓驶出车站。它在破旧的房屋和闪烁的河流中行进。在韦斯特兰车站，一群人挤在车门上，但乘务员把他们赶了出去，说这是专门为这个集市设计的火车。我一个人待在空旷的车厢里。几分钟后，火车就停在临时搭建的木制平台旁边。我走到路边，看到时钟的灯光表盘，还差十分钟到十点钟。在我面前是一座展示着神奇名字的大型建筑。

我找不到任何便宜的入

027

clock that it was ten minutes to ten. In front of me was a large building which displayed the magical name.

  I could not find any **sixpenny** entrance and, fearing that the bazaar would be closed, I passed in quickly through a turnstile, handing a shilling to a **weary**-looking man. I found myself in a big hall **girded** at half its height by a gallery. Nearly all the stalls were closed and the greater part of the hall was in darkness. I recognized a silence like that which pervades a church after a service. I walked into the centre of the bazaar timidly. A few people were gathered about the stalls which were still open. Before a curtain, over which the words Café Chantant were written in coloured lamps, two men were counting money on a salver. I listened to the fall of the coins.

口，担心市场会关闭，我迅速通过一个旋转门，向一个疲倦的男人交纳了一个先令。我发现自己坐在一个大厅里，一个画廊遮挡了它一半的高度。几乎所有的摊位都关门了，大部分大厅都是黑暗的。我意识到这种沉默就像经营过后弥漫在教堂里的那样。我小心翼翼地走进集市的中心。一些人聚集在仍然开放的摊位上。一张帷幕上，五颜六色的灯光凑成"Café Chantant"的字样，帷幕前，两个男人正在数托盘里的钱。我听着钱币落下的声音。

单词解析 Word Analysis

stride [straid] ▽ 大步走；阔步前进

例 He turned abruptly and strode off down the corridor.
  他突然转身，沿着走廊大步流星地走了。

throng [θrɔŋ] ▽ 群集；拥塞；拥向

例 Crowds thronged the stores.
  各商店都挤满了人。

draw up ▽ （车辆到达某处）停下，停止

例 The cab drew up outside the house.

出租车在房外停下了。

sixpenny [siks'pəni] *adj.* 便宜的；廉价的

例 It's a book he bought second-hand, years ago, off a sixpenny stall.
那是他多年前从一个廉价的书摊买的二手书。

weary ['wiəri] *adj.* 疲倦的；困乏的

例 She suddenly felt old and weary.
她突然感到一阵苍老和疲倦。

gird [gə:d] *v.* 束缚

例 Gird the loins of your mind.
约束你们的心。

语法知识点 Grammar Points

① The sight of the streets thronged with buyers and glaring with gas recalled to me the purpose of my journey.

本句话的主语是the street，谓语动词为recall。"thronged"和"glaring"皆为非谓语动词，一个表示被动：被挤满人；另一个则为主动，街道发着光。

"be thronged with sb./sth." 挤满（人、车辆等）

例 The streets were thronged with people.
条条大街都挤满了人。

② After an intolerable delay the train moved out of the station slowly.

"move out of" 移出……

例 Move out of my way!
让开！

③ I recognized a silence like that which pervades a church after a service.

此句话为which引导的定语从句，which代替a silence like that，并作从句的主语。

经典名句 Famous Classics

1. Ask much, know much.
   问的多，知道的多。

2. Believing in yourself is the secret of success.
   相信自己是成功的秘诀。

3. By other's faults wise man correct their own.
   前车之辙，后车可鉴。

4. You can make an enemy out of your best friend by lending him money.
   借钱给朋友，能使友成仇。

5. A clean fast is better than a dirty breakfast.
   宁为清贫，不为浊富。

6. Nightly prayer makes the day to shine.
   锁在笼子里的夜莺唱不出歌儿。（不能束缚人的思想。）

7. A chronic disease is difficult to treat.
   宿疾难医。

8. You can take a horse to the water, but you cannot make him drink.
   牵马河边易，逼其饮水难。（不要强人所难。）

9. By uniting we stand, by dividing we fall.
   团结则存，分裂则亡。

读书笔记

08 Clarissa
克拉丽莎

Indifferent as my head was, I had a little time to consider the man and his behavior. He terrified me with his looks, and with his violent emotions, as he gazed upon me. Evident joy — **suppressed** emotions, as I have since recollected. His sentences short, and pronounced as if his breath were touched. Never saw I his **abominable** eyes look as then they looked — triumph in them. — fierce and wild; and more disagreeable than the women's at the **vile** house appeared to me when I first saw them: and at times, such a **leering**, mischief-bodingcast. I would have given the world to have been a hundred miles from him. Yet his behaviour was decent — a decency, however, that I might have seen to be struggled for — for he **snatched** my hand two or three times, with a **vehemence** in his grasp that hurt me; speaking words of tenderness through his shut teeth, as it seemed; and let it go with a beggar — voiced humble accent; yet his words and manner carrying the appearance of strong and almost **convulsed** passion. Oh my dear. What

尽管我的头脑并不出众，但我还是有片刻时间来考虑这个人和他的举止。他盯着我时，他的表情、他狂暴的脾气都吓坏了我。犹记起，我是压抑快乐型性格，我一直如此。他的话很简短，他发出声音时，仿佛呼吸被阻碍着。当他们随后再看时，我从没见过他这么可恶的目光——他们成功了！——目光凶狠又野蛮；比我在邪恶的房屋中第一次见到的那些女人的目光更令人恶心；不时还投来些不怀好意、恶作剧的目光。如果可以的话，我宁愿离他有100英里远。他的举止是庄重的——还算客气，然而，我出于本能反抗起来——因为他有两三次抓住我的手，十分热情，但抓伤了我；他的言语很柔和，但他说话时似乎不张开嘴；更不用说他乞丐般的腔调了；然而他的话语和行为带着一种强烈到几乎震颤的热情！哦，天哪！他是多么罪恶，后来却不去反省。

我抱怨了一两次我口渴了。我想要水：他们给我一

mischiefs was he not then meditating.

　　I complained once or twice of thirst. I called for water: some table-beer was brought me: beer, I suppose, was a better vehicle (if I were not dosed enough before) for their potions. I told the maid that she knew I seldom tasted malt-liquor: yet, suspecting nothing of this nature, being extremely thirsty, I drank it and instantly, as it were, found myself much worse than before; as if inebriated, I should fancy: I know not how.

些轻啤酒：我想，啤酒，是他们加入他们药剂的不错工具（如果以前的剂量还不够大的话）。我和那个女仆说，她知道我以前很少喝麦芽酒：可是，我没有考虑我这种习惯，因为我实在太渴了，所以立刻喝下了酒。好像是当时，我就发现情况比以前更糟；我像喝醉了一样，我应该想想：我不知道怎么了。

单词解析 Word Analysis

indifferent [ɪnˈdɪfrənt] *adj.* 中等的

例 The festival has the usual mixture of movies— good, bad and indifferent .
电影节的影片一如既往地良莠不齐——有优秀的、低劣的和一般的。

suppress [səˈpres] *v.* 镇压，压制

例 She was unable to suppress her anger.
她按捺不住怒火。

abominable [əˈbɒmɪnəbl] *adj.* 讨厌的；可恶的

例 The judge described the attack as an abominable crime.
法官称那次袭击为令人发指的罪行。

vile [vaɪl] *adj.* 卑鄙的；粗鄙的，恶俗的

例 The weather was really vile most of the time.
天气大部分时间都糟糕得很。

leer [lɪər] *v.* 斜眼看

例 The invitation was plain, but not leering.
这邀请的用意显而易见，不过说得并不轻佻。

Clarissa 克拉丽莎 08

snatch [snætʃ] *v.* 抢夺，夺得

例 The magazine was snatch from my hand before I could read it.
我还没来得及看那期杂志，就被从我手里抢走了。

vehemence ['viːəməns] *n.* 热烈；强烈；猛烈；愤怒

例 She was astonished at his vehemence.
她对他的愤怒感到惊讶。

convulse [kən'vʌls] *v.* 使抽搐，使剧烈震动

例 A violent shiver convulsed him.
剧烈的颤抖使他抽搐不已。

语法知识点 Grammar Points

① **Indifferent as my head was, I had a little time to consider the man and his behavior.**

此句为"as"引导的让步状语从句，形容词提前，原来的顺序应为"As my head was indifferent"。

例 Intelligent as you are, I suspect you will fail.
尽管你聪明，我猜想你会失败。

② **Never saw I his abominable eyes look as then they looked — triumph in them. — fierce and wild; and more disagreeable than the women's at the vile house appeared to me when I first saw them: and at times, such a leering, mischief-bodingcast.**

"never"提前，要用倒装语序，原来的顺序应为"I never saw his abominable eyes look as then they looked"。

例 Never ever tell anyone your password.
不要把你的密码告诉任何人。

③ **I told the maid that she knew I seldom tasted malt-liquor: yet, suspecting nothing of this nature, being extremely thirsty, I drank it and instantly, as it were, found myself much worse than before; as if inebriated, I should fancy: I know not how.**

"that"引导宾语从句，"knew"后面实际上省略了一个that。

"as it were" 仿佛，好像，可以说

例 I'd understood the words, but I didn't, as it were, understand the question.
字面的意思我懂了，但是可以说我并不能理解这个问题。

经典名句 Famous Classics

1. Calamity is man's true touchstone.
   灾难是人生真正的试金石。

2. Call me not alive till you see me gathered.
   盖棺论定。

3. A bad husband makes a bad wife.
   有恶夫必有恶妻。（不是一家人，不进一家门。）

4. You cannot be too modest.
   人再怎么谦虚都不过分。（人越谦虚越好。）

5. You cannot burn the candle at both ends.
   蜡烛不能烧两头。（你不能经常熬夜。）

6. Preachers can talk but never teach, unless they practice what they preach.
   说教的人不身体力行，就只能空谈，不能起教育作用。

7. A blind man cannot judge colours.
   盲人不辨色。

8. A bird is known by its note and a man by his talk.
   鸟以声闻，人以言知。

读书笔记

09 Common Sense
常识

Society in every state is a blessing, but government even in its best state is but a necessary evil; in its worst state an intolerable one; for when we suffer, or are exposed to the same miseries by a government, which we might expect in a country without government, our calamity is heightened by reflecting that we **furnish** the means by which we suffer! Government, like dress, is the badge of lost innocence; the palaces of kings are built on the ruins of the **bowers** of paradise. For were the impulses of conscience clear, uniform, and irresistibly obeyed, man would need no other lawgiver; but that not being the case, he finds it necessary to surrender up a part of his property to furnish means for the protection of the rest; and this he is induced to do by the same prudence which in every other case advises him out of two evils to choose the least. Wherefore, security being the true design and end of government, it unanswerably follows that whatever form thereof appears most likely to ensure it to us, with the least expense and greatest benefit, is preferable to all

社会在各种情况下都是受人欢迎的，但是政府，即使在最好的情况下，也免不了是一个祸害；在最坏的情况下，就成了不可容忍的祸害；这是因为，当我们受苦的时候，当我们从一个政府那儿遭受了只有在无政府的国家中才可能遭受的不幸时，一想到是我们自己给自己带来了苦难，就格外痛心。政府好比衣服，象征着天真的流失；帝王的宫殿是建立在乐园的亭榭的废墟上的。如果良心的激发是日月可鉴、始终如一又忠贞不渝的，人类就无须其他的立法者；但事实并非如此，他必须交出一部分财产来换取对剩余财富的保护；谨慎小心的原则在其他任何场合都劝他两害相权取其轻，现在这个原则也促使他这样做。因此，既然安全是政府的真正的意图和目的，那就可以毫无疑义地推断，任何看起来最有可能保证我们安全的形式，只要是花费最少而得益最大，人都是愿意接受的。

为了清晰准确地了解政

others.

In order to gain a clear and just idea of the design and end of government, let us suppose a small number of persons settled in some **sequestered** part of the earth, unconnected with the rest, they will then represent the first peopling of any country, or of the world. In this state of natural liberty, society will be their first thought. A thousand motives will excite them thereto, the strength of one man is so unequal to his wants, and his mind so unfitted for perpetual solitude, that he **is soon obliged to** seek assistance and relief of another, who in his turn requires the same. Four or five united would be able to raise a tolerable dwelling in the midst of a wilderness, but one man might labor out the common period of life without accomplishing any thing; when he had felled his **timber** he could not remove it, nor erect it after it was removed; hunger in the mean time would urge him from his work, and every different want call him a different way. Disease, **nay** even misfortune would be death, for though neither might be mortal, yet either would disable him from living, and reduce him to a state in which he might rather be said to perish than to die.

府的意图和目的，我们假定有一部分人在地球的某一个隐僻的地方住下来，同其余的人不发生联系，他们就将代表任何一块地方或世界上的第一批移民。在这种自然的自由状态下，他们首先想到的将会是社会。千百种的动机都将鼓励他们趋向这一目标。单单一个人的力量满足不了他的需求，他的心境又不甘永远孤独，因此他不久后就必须从另一个人那儿得到帮助和安慰，而对方也有同样的需要。四五个人通力合作，就能够在旷野当中兴建一个勉强凑合的住所，但单靠一个人的力量可能劳碌终生也一事无成。砍完了木头搬不动，就是搬动了也搭建不起来；同时饥饿会逼他停止工作，每一种不同的需要会以不同的方式来支配着他。疾病，而且不幸还意味着死亡；尽管它们并不致死，但也会使他不能维持生活，落到与其说是死亡不如说是毁灭的境地。

单词解析 Word Analysis

furnish ['fɜːnɪʃ] *v.* 提供，供应；陈设，布置

例 She furnished him with the facts surrounding the case.
她向他提供了与案件有关的事实。

bower ['baʊə(r)] *n.* 凉亭，阴凉处

例 He sat in the bower to have a seat.
他坐在凉亭里休息一下。

sequestered [sɪ'kwestəd] *adj.* 隐退的；幽静的；偏僻的

例 She knew sequestered spots where the hens laid their eggs.
他知道母鸡在什么隐蔽的地方下蛋。

be obliged to *v.* 不得不；必须；只好

例 She is obliged to abandon her idea of trying again.
她不得不放弃再试试的想法。

timber ['tɪmbə(r)] *n.* 木材，木料

例 The fire has burned up 18,000 acres of timber.
那场大火烧光了1.8万英亩的木材。

nay [neɪ] *adv.* 不仅如此；而且

例 Such a policy is difficult, nay impossible.
这一政策很难实施，甚至是不可能的。

语法知识点 Grammar Points

① **Government, like dress, is the badge of lost innocence; the palaces of kings are built on the ruins of the bowers of paradise.**

"like dress" 为插入语，并在此处涉及了明喻（simile）的修辞手法。

例 I rushed to the dining room like a hungry bear.
我像饿狼扑食般冲向食堂。

例 She is as red as a rose.
她面若桃花。

"be built on" 以……为基础，建立在……之上

例 A good relationship is built on honesty, trust, and mutual respect.
良好的关系建立在诚实、信任和相互尊敬之上。

② **For were the impulses of conscience clear, uniform, and irresistibly obeyed, man would need no other lawgiver; but that not being the case, he finds it necessary to surrender up a part of his property to furnish means for the protection of the rest.**

此句话为由for引导的原因状语从句，句子的主句为"man would need no other lawgiver"，从句中又涉及由if引导的条件状语从句，在虚拟语气中的从句中出现were、should、had时，if可省略，同时把were/should/had放在句首，形成倒装句。原句的语序为："If the impulses of conscience were clear, uniform, and irresistibly obeyed..."。

例 Were she a man, she might be elected president.
如果她是男人，就能被选为总统。

③ **Wherefore, security being the true design and end of government, it unanswerably follows that whatever form thereof appears most likely to ensure it to us, with the least expense and greatest benefit, is preferable to all others.**

"security being the true design and end of government"是独立主格结构，此句真正的主语是it，谓语动词是follows。

例 The meeting being over, all of us went home.
开完会我们都回家了。

经典名句 Famous Classics

1. You cannot catch old birds with chaff.
   用糠做诱饵捉不住老鸟。（姜还是老的辣。）

2. You cannot eat your cake and have your cake.
   两者不可兼得。

3. You cannot get blood out of a stone.
   你不可能从铁石心肠的人那里求得帮助。

4. You cannot get leave to thrive for throng.
   心急吃不了热豆腐。（欲速则不达。）

5. Care and diligence bring luck.
   谨慎和勤奋带来好运。

6. Care is enemy to health.
   忧虑乃健康之敌。

7. Opportunity seldom knocks twice.
   机遇很少敲两次门。（机不可失，时不再来。）

8. A bad life, a bad end.
   恶有恶报。

9. One today is worth two tomorrows.
   一个今天胜似两个明天。

读书笔记

10 Death of a Salesman
推销员之死

Willy Loman, a sixty-year-old traveling salesman, enters his home late at night with two large sample cases. His wife, Linda, hears him coming up the stairs to their bedroom. She seems worried that something has happened, that he has **wrecked** the car again, or that he's ill, but Willy assures her that he is fine, just tired. Sitting on the bed with her, he explains that he came home because he was having trouble staying on the road while he drove, and he is unsure of what caused his distraction. It could've been the coffee he had at a roadside diner or the way he opened the windshield of the car and the scenery and sunshine just washed over him. Whatever it was, it kept taking his mind of the road, and he'd **veer** onto the shoulder before he knew what was happening. He was so **spooked** that he drove ten miles an hour all the way home, and now he's tired and **grumpy** because he's going to miss his morning meeting in Portland, Rhode Island. Linda urges him to talk to his boss about working in the New York area so that he doesn't have to travel anymore,

一位六十岁的旅行推销员威利·洛曼深夜拎着两个沉重的、装着样品的箱子回到家。他的妻子琳达听到他上楼梯，走到了他们的卧室。她似乎担心发生了什么事，担心他再次破坏了车子或是他生病了，但威利向她保证他没事，只是累了。他们一起坐在床上，威利向妻子解释说他回家是因为他在开车时遇到了麻烦，他不确定是什么让他分心。这可能是他在路边餐厅用过的咖啡，或者是他打开汽车挡风玻璃风景和阳光恰恰笼罩着他。不管原因是什么，他一直在考虑这条路，在他还没有弄清楚原因前，他已经把注意力转向肩膀。他非常惊讶自己回来时的车速是每小时十英里。一想到自己会错过开在罗德岛波特兰的晨间会议，他就感到疲倦又暴躁。琳达劝他与他的老板谈谈在纽约地区工作，以便他不必再旅行出差了，但他对她说：“纽约不需要我。我是新英格兰人。我对新英格兰地区至关重要。”针对他应该在纽

but he says to her, "They don't need me in New York. I'm the New England man. I'm vital in New England." After more discussion of all the reasons why he should be working in New York, Linda suggests again that he go speak with his boss, Howard Wagner, Willy finally agrees to do it, emphasizing that if Wagner's father were still in charge of the company, Willy would have already had a New York job. Wagner doesn't appreciate Willy the way his father did.

约工作的所有理由进行更多的讨论之后，琳达再次建议他与他的老板霍华德·瓦格纳谈谈，最终，威利同意这么做，强调如果瓦格纳父亲仍然负责该公司，威利早就有了一份纽约的工作。瓦格纳并不像他父亲那样欣赏威利。

单词解析 Word Analysis

wreck [rek] v. 破坏，毁坏

例 The building had been wrecked by the explosion.
那座楼房被炸毁了。

veer [vɪə(r)] v.（尤指交通工具）改变方向或路线

例 The bus veered onto the wrong side of the road.
公共汽车突然驶入了逆行道。

spooked [spuːkt] adj. 吓坏的

例 He was so spooked that he, too, began to believe that he heard strange clicks and noises on their telephones.
他太害怕了，以至于也开始相信自己听到了他们的电话发出奇怪的咔嗒声响。

grumpy ['grʌmpi] adj. 脾气坏的；性情粗暴的

例 Don't be so grumpy and cynical about it.
不要为此这么生气，这么愤世嫉俗。

语法知识点 Grammar Points

① **She seems worried that something has happened, that he has wrecked the car again, or that he's ill, but Willy assures her that he is fine, just tired.**

此句中的前3个"that"都引导宾语从句，表并列。"but Willy assures her that"中的that也引导宾语从句。"assure that"保证。

例 He hastened to assure that the press would not be informed.
他急忙保证新闻界是不会知道的。

② **Sitting on the bed with her, he explains that he came home because he was having trouble staying on the road while he drove, and he is unsure of what caused his distraction.**

"Sitting on the bed with her"至于句首，现在分词作伴随状语。

例 Hearing a strange sound, he went out of the house.
他听到了奇怪的声音就出来了。

③ **After more discussion of all the reasons why he should be working in New York, Linda suggests again that he go speak with his boss, Howard Wagner, Willy finally agrees to do it, emphasizing that if Wagner's father were still in charge of the company, Willy would have already had a New York job.**

"why"引导原因状语从句，对reasons进行进一步解释说明。

例 There is no earthly reason why they should ever change.
他们完全没有必要做出改变。

"suggest"为"建议"之意时，后接that引导的宾语从句时，动词形式应为should do, 其中should可省。

例 I suggest that we go out to eat.
我提议我们出去吃吧。

经典名句 Famous Classics

1. Catch the hare before you cook him.
先捉兔子后下锅。

2. Character is the first and last word in the success circle.
   人的品德是事业成功的决定条件。

3. You cannot whistle and drink at the same time.
   你不能边吹口哨边喝茶。（人不能干两件截然相反的事。）

4. Children have the qualities of the parents.
   有什么样的父母，就有什么样的孩子。

5. Pardon makes offenders.
   姑息养奸。

6. Pain is gain.
   痛苦即是收获。（痛苦中有教益。）

7. A bad conscience is a snake in one's heart.
   做贼心虚。

8. One sows another reaps.
   播种和收割的未必是同一个人。（享受者未必是应该享受的那个人。）

9. A beggar's scrip is never filled.
   乞丐的口袋是填不满的。（乞丐无足时。）

读书笔记

11 Emma
爱玛

Emma Woodhouse, handsome, clever, and rich, with a comfortable home and happy **disposition**, seemed to unite some of the best blessing of existence; and had lived nearly twenty-one years in the world with very little to distress or **vex** her.

She was the youngest of the two daughters of a most **affectionate**, **indulgent** father; and had, in consequence of her sister's marriage, been mistress of his house from a very early period. Her mother had died too long ago for her to have more than an indistinct remembrance of her **caresses**; and her place had been supplied by an excellent woman as **governess**, who had fallen little short of a mother in affection.

Sixteen years had Miss Taylor been in Mr. Woodhouse's family, less as a governess than a friend, very fond of both daughters, but particularly of Emma. Between them it was more the intimacy of sisters. Even before Miss Taylor had ceased to hold the nominal office of governess, the mildness of her temper had hardly allowed her to impose any restraint; and the shadow of

爱玛·伍德豪斯端庄儒雅、聪慧过人、家境富裕，加上家庭温暖、性格开朗，仿佛人生的几大福分让她占全了。在她将近二十一年的花样年华中，极少出现苦恼烦心的事情。

爱玛有个极其慈爱的父亲。他对两个女儿十分娇惯宠溺，而爱玛又是他的小女儿。姐姐出嫁后，爱玛小小年纪就担当了家庭女主人的角色。母亲去世得太早，她的爱抚，爱玛只模模糊糊记得一点儿。一位杰出的家庭女教师填补了母亲的空缺，她对爱玛的慈爱之心不亚于一个母亲。

泰勒小姐在伍德豪斯先生家生活了十六年，她不仅仅是孩子们的家庭教师，更是她们的朋友。她非常疼爱两个姑娘，特别是爱玛。她俩之间情同姐妹。泰勒小姐性情温和，甚至在她名义上还担任家庭教师时，也很少去管束爱玛。后来师生关系彻底消失了，两人就像知心闺蜜一样生活在一起，爱玛更是爱做什么就做什么。她十分尊重泰勒小姐的意见，但她主

authority being now long passed away, they had been living together as friend and friend very mutually attached, and Emma doing just what she liked; highly **esteeming** Miss Taylor's judgment, but directed chiefly by her own.

The real evils, indeed, of Emma's situation were the power of having rather too much her own way, and a disposition to think a little too well of herself; these were the disadvantages which threatened alloy to her many enjoyments. The danger, however, was at present so unperceived, that they did not by any means rank as misfortunes with her.

要按自己的心意行事。

要说爱玛的境况真有什么危害的话，那就是她太随心所欲了，还有点自视过高，这些可能会减少许多乐趣，是不利因素。不过，目前这种危险尚未显现，对她来说还算不上什么不幸。

单词解析 Word Analysis

disposition [ˌdɪspəˈzɪʃn] *n.* 性情，性格

例 She has shown no abnormality in intelligence or in disposition.
她在智力或性情上都未显示出任何反常。

vex [veks] *v.* 使苦恼；使生气

例 I didn't think to vex you by such a trifle.
我根本没想到你会因为这点小事而生气。

affectionate [əˈfekʃənət] *adj.* 慈爱的

例 He is very affectionate towards his children.
他非常疼爱他的孩子。

indulgent [ɪnˈdʌldʒənt] *adj.* 放纵的，纵容的

例 He was an indulgent father, ever ready to provide new clothes.
他是个溺爱的父亲，随时乐意给孩子买新衣服。

045

我的名著美文：人不是生来就要被打败的

caress [kəˈres] *n.* 爱抚，抚摸

例 The caresses of the breeze played over his face.
微风轻轻拂过他的脸庞。

governess [ˈgʌvənəs] *n.* 女家庭教师

例 He does not like the new governess by a fraction.
他一点也不喜欢他的新家庭女教师。

esteem [ɪˈstiːm] *v.* 尊敬，敬重

例 She was esteemed the perfect novelist.
她被认为是最完美的小说家。

语法知识点 Grammar Points

① She was the youngest of the two daughters of a most affectionate, indulgent father; and had, in consequence of her sister's marriage, been mistress of his house from a very early period.

此句为由"；"连接的两个小并列句组成。"in consequence of"由于，是……的结果；在本句中作插入语。

例 In consequence of his bad work, I was forced to dismiss him.
由于他工作表现不好，我只好把他辞退。

② Her mother had died too long ago for her to have more than an indistinct remembrance of her caresses; and her place had been supplied by an excellent woman as governess, who had fallen little short of a mother in affection.

"more than +n." 只不过……

例 Their replies were no more than grunts of acknowledgement.
他们所谓的回答不过是表示承认的"咕哝"罢了。

"be supplied by" 由……提供；由……供应

例 We are supplied with vegetables by nearby farmers.
附近的农民供应我们蔬菜。

046

③ **Even before Miss Taylor had ceased to hold the nominal office of governess, the mildness of her temper had hardly allowed her to impose any restraint.**

"even" 即使，甚至；引导让步状语从句。"before" 在……之前，引导时间状语从句，从句用一般过去时，主句用过去完成时。

例 Before I got to the bus stop, the bus had left.
在我到达公共汽车站前，公共汽车已经开走了。

④ **The danger, however, was at present so unperceived, that they did not by any means rank as misfortunes with her.**

"by any means" 无论如何

例 She is by no means an inexperienced teacher.
她绝不是个毫无经验的教师。

"rank as" 把……看作；可算作……

例 It certainly doesn't rank as his greatest win.
这肯定算不上他最大的胜利。

经典名句 Famous Classics

1. Constancy is the foundation of virtue.
   恒心是美德的基础。

2. You have made your bed, you must lie in it.
   自己铺的床自己躺。（自作自受。/自食其果。）

3. Content is happiness.
   知足常乐。

4. Conversation makes one what he is.
   言如其人。

5. You have no goats, and yet you sell kids.
   家中无老羊，轮到卖羊羔。

6. You may as well be hanged for a sheep as a lamb.
   大偷、小偷都是偷。

7. You may delay, but time will not.
   人拖时不拖。（岁月不待人。）

8. A candle lights others and consumes itself.
   蜡烛焚自身，光亮照别人。

读书笔记

12 For Whom the Bell Tolls
丧钟为谁而鸣

His mind wanders. He knows that that he must use people he likes as **troops**, and tries to convince himself that he has no responsibility for them; he is only obeying Golz's orders. He thinks of another commander, the swine Gomez in Estremadura. He believes that the **partizans** bring bad luck and danger, but make the country a good place in which to live. He feels conflicted and **worries about** betraying the people. He fights because he loves Spain. He fights with the communists only for the duration of the war, for it is the only group he can respect. He knows he cannot tell anyone that he has no politics. He wonders about Pablo's politics, and decides he probably moved from left to right, having only faith in ultimate victory: the politics of horse thieves. "Was there ever a people whose leaders were as truly their enemies as this one?" He has become **bigoted** from politics, and his mind too easily uses clichés like "enemy of the people".

Robert Jordan does not want to be a hero or a **martyr**, and just wants to spend a long time with Maria. The

他的思绪飘向远方。他知道他必须用他欣赏的人组成军队，他试着说服自己：他只是在遵循上帝的旨意行事，对他们不负有任何责任。他想起了另一位指挥官——在埃斯特雷马杜拉的讨厌鬼戈麦斯。他认为党派给国家带来了厄运和危险，但同时使它成为了适合居住的好地方。他觉得很矛盾，很怕自己背叛人民。他选择战斗是因为他热爱西班牙。他只有在战争期间才会与共产党人为敌，因为那是他唯一可以尊敬的团体。他知道决不能告诉任何人他没有政治信仰。他想知道巴勃罗的政治信仰，很可能他从左派转移到右派，唯一的目标就是最终的胜利：偷马贼政策。"人民的领导者是人民真正的敌人，世界上哪个国家有过这样的情况？"在政治上，他很偏执，因此像"人民的敌人"这种陈词滥调是没有多加考虑就涌上心头的。

罗伯特·乔丹不想做英雄或者烈士，他只想和玛利亚共度悠长的岁月。当他的内疚感占

marriage fantasy he sets up becomes cynical as his guilt takes over, for he knows that he can take her with him, but he cannot change what happened to her.

……

He knows that he came upon her late, but their connection is so strong that they would have come together even if Pilar had not **intervened**. However, her intervention saved precious time. He **berates** himself for the impossible fantasy of having a long life with Maria, and knows the urgency of the time they have.

据上风时，他便怀疑关于婚姻自己构建起来的幻想，因为他知道他可以把玛利亚带在身边却不能改变在她身上发生的事情。

……

他知道他们相遇得较晚，但他们彼此是那样的心意相通以至于就算没有比拉尔的干涉他们也会走到一起。不过比拉尔为他们节省下了宝贵的时间。他严厉斥责自己和玛利亚共度余生的幻想，他知道他们所剩下的时间不多了。

单词解析 Word Analysis

troop [tru:p] *n.* 军队，部队

例 The president decided to send in the troops.
总统决定派遣军队。

partizan [ˌpɑːtiˈzæn] *n.* 党派，党人

例 At first the eager young poet was a partizan of Revolution.
起初，那位满腔热血的年轻人是革命的支持者。

worry about *v.* 担忧，担心

例 He's always worrying about his weight.
他一直为体重而发愁。

bigoted [ˈbɪɡətɪd] *adj.* 偏执的，顽固的

例 He was bigoted and racist.
他非常偏执而且有种族歧视的思想。

martyr [ˈmɑːtə(r)] *n.* 烈士

例 If he dies, he will be a martyr.

For Whom the Bell Tolls 丧钟为谁而鸣 12

如果他牺牲了，他就是一名烈士了。

intervene [ˌɪntəˈviːn] 介入；阻碍，干扰

例 They were planning to get married and then the war intervened.
他们正准备结婚，不巧被战事耽搁了。

berate [bɪˈreɪt] 严责；申斥

例 From that moment on, I knew I would never berate my son for imperfect grades.
从那一刻起，我就知道自己再也不会因为儿子的成绩不理想而去斥责他。

语法知识点 Grammar Points

① **He knows that that he must use people he likes as troops, and tries to convince himself that he has no responsibility for them; he is only obeying Golz's orders.**

"convince oneself that" "说服自己……、劝服自己……"，后接宾语从句。

例 I convince myself that everything will be fine.
我劝自己一切都会好起来的。

"have no responsibility for" 不对……承担责任

例 The bank refuses to accept responsibility for the mistake.
银行拒绝为这个错误承担责任。

② **The marriage fantasy he sets up becomes cynical as his guilt takes over, for he knows that he can take her with him, but he cannot change what happened to her.**

本句运用了较多的状语从句：由as引导的时间状语从句和for引导的原因状语从句。连词but引导两个句子，表转折。
此句中实际上省略了fantasy后面定语从句的引导词that，完整的应为"The marriage fantasy that he sets up,"作整个句子的主语。"set up sth./set sth. up""建立，建起"。

例 The police set up roadblocks on routes out of the city.
警察在城外设了路障。

051

"take over sth./take sth. over" 接任，接管；控制

例 When the main system fails, the backup system takes over.
当主系统不能工作后，备用系统会接管其工作。

③ **He knows that he came upon her late, but their connection is so strong that they would have come together even if Pilar had not intervened.**

"come upon/on sb." 偶然遇到；偶然发现

例 I've come upon the word for several times.
我已经碰到这个单词好几次了。

"would have done + even if" 的结构为让步状语从句下的虚拟语气，可译为"即使……也会"。

例 He would have done well even if she had not helped him.
即使没有她帮助，他也会做得非常好的。

经典名句 Famous Classics

1. Courtesy on one side only lasts not long.
   来而不往非礼也。

2. You make the failure complete when you stop trying.
   不再努力之时，就是完全失败之日。

3. Covetousness is the root of all evil.
   贪婪为万恶之源。

4. Creep before you walk.
   循序渐进。

5. Custom is a second nature.
   习惯是第二天性。

6. Custom is the guide of the ignorant.
   习俗是无知者的向导。

7. You scratch my back and I'll scratch yours.
   相互利用，狼狈为奸。

13 Gone with the Wind
飘

She had **gone back to** Tara once in fear and defeat and she had emerged from its sheltering walls strong and armed for victory. What she had done once, somehow—please God, she could do again! How, she did not know. She did not want to think of that now. All she wanted was a breathing space in which to hurt, a quiet place to lick her wounds, a **haven** in which to plan her campaign. She thought of Tara and it was as if a gentle cool hand were **stealing over** her heart. She could see the white house **gleaming** welcome to her through the reddening autumn leaves, feel the quiet hush of the country twilight coming down over her like a **benediction**, feel the dews falling on the acres of green bushes starred with **fleecy** white, see the raw color of the red earth and the dismal dark beauty of the pines on the rolling hills.

She felt vaguely comforted, strengthened by the picture, and some of her hurt and frantic regret was pushed from the top of her mind. She stood for a moment remembering small things, the avenue of dark cedars leading to Tara,

她曾经怀着惶恐和沮丧的心情回到塔拉去，后来在它的庇护下恢复了坚强，再次武装起来，重新投入战斗。只要是她曾经历过的，无论怎样——请上帝保佑，她能够再来一次！她不知道要怎样做。她现在不想考虑这些。她想要的仅仅是一个喘息的机会来熬过痛苦、一个宁静的地方来舔舐伤口、一个避难所来计划下一次战役。她一想到塔拉就像有一只温柔而又能令她冷静的手在安抚她的心灵。她看得见那幢白得发亮的房子在转红的秋树叶的掩映下向她招手欢迎；感觉得到乡下黄昏时的宁静安谧像祝祷一样笼罩着她；感觉得到落在绿色的灌木丛里似羊毛白般的露水；看得见跌宕起伏的山丘上那些原生态的红土地和忧郁又美丽的松树。

她从这幅图景中得到了鼓舞，内心了隐隐地感到宽慰，因此也减轻了一些心头的痛苦和悔恨。她站了一会来回忆一些小细节，如：通向塔拉的那条种满雪松的林荫道、在白墙

the banks of cape jessamine bushes, vivid green against the white walls, the **fluttering** white curtains. And Mammy would be there. Suddenly she wanted Mammy desperately, as she had wanted her when she was a little girl, wanted the broad bosom on which to lay her head, the **gnarled** black hand on her hair. Mammy, the last link with the old days.

With the spirit of her people who would not know defeat, even when it **stared them in the face**, she raised her chin. She could get Rhett back. She knew she could. There had never been a man she couldn't get, once she set her mind upon him.

"I'll think of it all tomorrow, at Tara. I can stand it then. Tomorrow, I'll think of some way to get him back. After all, tomorrow is another day."

的映衬下鲜绿的茉莉花丛以及挥舞着的白色窗帘。嬷嬷一定在那里。她突然迫切地想见嬷嬷了，就像她小时候需要她那样，需要她那宽阔的胸膛，让她好把自己的头伏在上面，需要她那双因劳累而变形的黑手来抚摩她的头发。嬷嬷是她与过去最后的联系。

她具有她的家族那种即使失败就摆在眼前也不认输的精神，她会把下巴高高翘起。她能够把瑞德回来。她知道她可以。只要她下定决心，世界上没有哪个男人她无法得到。

"我明天回塔拉再去想吧。那时我就承受得住一切了。明天，我会想出个办法把他弄回来。毕竟，明天又是新的一天（开始）。"

单词解析 *Word Analysis*

go back to 回去；归

例 I'm not ready to go back to work yet.
我还没准备回去工作。

haven ['heivn] 港口，避难所

例 The hotel is a haven of peace and tranquility.
这家旅店是一个安宁的去处。

steal over 不知不觉地向……袭来，对……产生影响

例 Pallor began to steal over his features.
一阵苍白开始袭向他的脸庞。

gleam [gli:m] v.（使）闪烁，（使）闪亮

例 The moonlight gleamed on the water.
月光照在湖面上，泛起粼粼波光。

benediction [,beni'diʃn] n.（基督教的）祝福，祝祷

例 She could only raise her hand in a gesture of benediction.
她只得举起手来做一个祝福的手势。

fleecy ['fli:si] n. 软如羊毛的，羊毛似的

例 The fleecy clouds sailed across the sky.
白云飘过天空。

flutter ['flʌtə(r)] v.（使）挥动，舞动

例 He fluttered his hands around wildly.
他使劲儿挥舞着双手。

gnarled [na:ld] adj. 扭曲的，多节瘤的

例 The tree has gnarled red branches and deep green leaves.
这棵树的枝干扭曲且呈红色，树叶则为深绿色。

stare in the face 盯着，直视，显而易见，就在眼前

例 Defeat was staring them in the face.
他们必遭失败。

语法知识点 Grammar Points

① All she wanted was a breathing space in which to hurt, a quiet place to lick her wounds, a haven in which to plan her campaign.

"all she wanted" 作整句话的主语，省略了定语从句的引导词that，应为 "all that she wanted"。表语是三个并列的名词短语：a breathing space..., a quiet place..., a haven...。在这三个并列的表语中，"in which" 表示 "在……地方"。

② **She thought of Tara and it was as if a gentle cool hand were stealing over her heart.**

"think of" "考虑，想起"，后可直接加名词作宾语。

例 I can't think of her name at the moment.
　　我一时想不起她的名字。

"as if" "好像，仿佛"，在本句中引导表语从句，从句用虚拟语气。

例 It's as if I'm living in a hazy dream world.
　　我好像活在缥缈的梦里。

③ **Suddenly she wanted Mammy desperately, as she had wanted her when she was a little girl, wanted the broad bosom on which to lay her head, the gnarled black hand on her hair.**

"as" "正如，正像"，引导方式状语从句。"wanted Mammy desperately" 和 "wanted the broad bosom…" 为两个并列的动词词组，"the broad bosom" 和 "the gnarled black hand" 同为第二个 wanted 的宾语。

经典名句 Famous Classics

1. A casual remark sounds significant to a suspicious listener.
   说者无心，听者有意。

2. Civility costs nothing.
   礼貌不需什么代价。

3. You dig your grave with your teeth.
   用牙齿挖自己的坟墓。（自掘坟墓，自食其果。）

4. Death for a common cause is beautiful.
   为人民事业而死，死得其所。

5. You have dived deep into the water and have brought up a pot shred.
   潜入深水里，却捞出碎瓷片。（无功而返。）

6. Conceit comes from shallowness; arrogance is due to ignorance.
   骄傲来自浅薄，狂妄出于无知。

7. You go your way, I'll go mine.
   你走你的阳关道，我过我的独木桥。（我们各走各的路，互不相干。）

8. Danger past, God forgotten.
   过河拆桥。

读书笔记

14 Great Expectations
远大前程

In every rage of wind and rush of rain, I heard pursuers. Twice, I could have sworn there was a knocking and whispering at the outer door. With these fears upon me, I began either to imagine or recall that I had had mysterious warnings of this man's approach. That, for weeks gone by, I had passed faces in the streets which I had thought like his. That, these likenesses had grown more numerous, as he, coming over the sea, had drawn nearer. That, his **wicked** spirit had somehow sent these messengers to mine, and that now on this stormy night he was as good as his word, and with me.

Crowding up with these reflections came the reflection that I had seen him with my childish eyes to be a desperately violent man; that I had heard that other **convict reiterate** that he had tried to murder him; that I had seen him down in the ditch tearing and fighting like a wild beast. Out of such **remembrances** I brought into the light of fire, a half-formed terror that it might not be safe to be shut up there with him in the dead of the wild solitary night.

屋外的阵阵狂风怒吼声和唰唰的雨点声中夹杂着追捕的声音。有两次，我确信自己听到外面有敲门声和低低的说话声。我心头堆满了恐惧，于是一些想象和回忆都涌上心头，好像出现过些神秘的预警，预示着他的到来。在过去的几周内，我在街上就遇到过不少和他极为相似的人。就在他越过重洋，距我越来越近的时候，和他相似的人也就越来越多。他那邪恶的灵魂把这些信使送到我身边，如今在这狂风暴雨之夜，他果然信守诺言，来到我的身边。

随着我渐渐长大，对他的印象不断累积，好像他在我童年时期那天真的眼中就是一个不顾死活性格暴躁的人；我曾亲耳听到另一个逃犯细数说着要杀害他的阴谋；我曾亲眼看到他在深深的沟渠中像一头野兽似的和别人撕扯扭打。我跳出回忆，把注意力放在火光上，仿佛出现了一个极为可怕的影子——在这个狂风暴雨之夜，在这个寂静孤独之夜，了

This **dilated** until it filled the room, and **impelled** me to take a candle and go in and look at my dreadful burden.

He had rolled a handkerchief round his head, and his face was set and lowering in his sleep. But he was asleep, and quietly too, though he had a pistol lying on the pillow. Assured of this, I softly removed the key to the outside of his door, and turned it on him before I again sat down by the fire. Gradually I slipped from the chair and lay on the floor. When I awoke, without having parted in my sleep with the perception of my **wretchedness**, the clocks of the Eastward churches were striking five, the candles were wasted out, the fire was dead, and the wind and rain intensified the thick black darkness.

无生气,和他待在一起怕是不安全吧。这个可怕的影子渐渐扩大,直到充满了整个房间,使我不得不端起烛台走到里面去查看一下我那可怕的包袱。

他睡在那里,头上扎了一条手帕,头部压得很低,一动不动的。他正沉沉地睡着,很安静,不过枕旁放着一把手枪。我这才放心,轻轻地把房门的钥匙拔出插到外面,反锁了门,才又坐回到炉边。慢慢地我从椅子上滑落到地板上。待我醒来时,东面教堂的钟敲了五下,蜡烛已经燃尽,炉火也早已全熄,屋外的狂风暴雨使夜色更加黑暗浓郁了,而我仍沉浸在梦里的忧伤之中。

单词解析 Word Analysis

wicked ['wikid] *adj.* 邪恶的

例 He has a wicked sense of humor.
他有一种恶作剧的幽默感。

convict [kən'vikt] *n.* 罪犯

例 The escaped convict was seized outside the city.
逃犯在城外被抓。

reiterate [ri'itəreit] *v.* 重申,复述

例 The boy did not move though the teacher reiterated her command.
虽然教师重申命令,那个男孩也不动。

remembrance [ri'membrəns] *n.* 记忆力；记忆

例 They wore black in remembrance of those who had died.
他们身穿黑色衣服，以纪念那些亡故者。

dilate [dai'leit] *v.* 扩大

例 Red wine can help dilate blood vessels.
红酒有助于血管扩张。

impel [im'pel] *v.* 促使；迫使

例 There are various reasons that impel me to that conclusion.
各种各样的原因促使我得出那个结论。

wretchedness ['retʃidnəs] *n.* 可怜，悲惨

例 She deserves some good luck after so much wretchedness.
在经历这么多不幸后，她值得拥有好运气。

语法知识点 Grammar Points

① **With these fears upon me, I began either to imagine or recall that I had had mysterious warnings of this man's approach.**

"With these fears upon me" 作伴随状语，表示状态。

例 He lay on the bed with the bedroom door shut.
他躺在床上，卧室门关着。

② **Out of such remembrances I brought into the light of fire, a half-formed terror that it might not be safe to be shut up there with him in the dead of the wild solitary night.**

"the wild solitary night" 此短语涉及了移就（Transferred Epithet）的修辞手法；solitary是"孤单的，孤独的"意思，表面上修饰night，实际上修饰的是人。

例 He has spent several sleepless nights.
他度过了几个失眠夜。（sleepless实际上修饰的是主语He，而不是nights）

He lent a patient ear to hear her story.
他耐心地听她讲述着她的事。（patient实际上修饰的并非ear，而是He）

③ Assured of this, I softly removed the key to the outside of his door, and turned it on him before I again sat down by the fire.

"be assured of" 确信

例 I am assured that something is going wrong.
我确信现在出了什么差错。

经典名句 Famous Classics

1. Young saints, old devils.
   少时是圣徒，大时成魔鬼。（少时圣洁老邪恶。）

2. Your conversation is the mirror of your thoughts.
   言语是心灵的镜子。（言为心声。）

3. The dog that is idle barks at his fleas, but he that is hunting feels them not.
   懒狗才会抱怨自己身上的虱子，勤快的狗是察觉不到虱子的。

4. Your money burns (a hole) in your pocket.
   钱烧口袋漏，一有就不留。

5. Custom reconciles us to everything.
   习惯使人安于一切。

6. Cut off a dog's tail and he will be a dog still.
   小损失无碍大局。

7. Debt is the worst kind of poverty.
   负债是最糟糕的贫穷。

8. Deliberate in counsel, prompt in action.
   考虑要仔细，行动要迅速。

9. The dust raised by the sheep does not choke the wolf.
   羊踩起的灰尘挡不住狼。

15 Hard Times
艰难时世

Now what I want is, Facts. Teach these boys and girls nothing but Facts. Facts alone are wanted in life. Plant nothing else, and root out everything else. You can only form the minds of reasoning animals upon Facts: nothing else will ever be of any service to them. This is the principle on which I bring up my own children, and this is the principle on which I bring up these children. Stick to Facts, sir!

The scene was a plain, bare, monotonous **vault** of a school-room, and the speaker's square forefinger emphasized his observations by understanding every sentence with a line on the schoolmaster's sleeve. The emphasis was helped by the speaker's square wall of a forehead, which had his eyebrows for its base, while his eyes found **commodious** cellarage in two dark caves, overshadowed by the wall. The emphasis was helped by the speaker's mouth, which was wide, thin, and hard set. The emphasis was helped by the speaker's voice, which was inflexible, dry, and **dictatorial**. The emphasis was helped by the speaker's

现在我想要的是事实。除了事实，不要教这些男孩和女孩任何别的东西。生活唯一需要的只有事实。别培育其他任何事物，根除一切其他事物。你只能通过事实形成具有推理能力的动物头脑：其他一切都用不上。这是我抚养孩子的原则，这也是我培养这些孩子的原则。坚持事实，先生！

这是一间简陋单调的拱形教室，屋里没什么陈设。讲话的人每次说完一句话，就用他那方方正正的食指在那位教师的袖子上横划一下，来加强语气。说话者那宽大如墙一般的前额帮助加强语气，而前额这堵墙以他的眉毛作基地，眼睛在被墙掩盖着的两个黑暗的洞穴中发现了宽敞的容身之处。说话者那又宽又薄又坚硬的嘴巴加强了这种语气；说话者那呆板、无聊又蛮横的声音加强了这种语气；说话者那秃头边上竖着的也加强了这种语气。他的头发像种植的冷杉为发亮的顶部抵挡大风，顶部的凹凸不平，就像葡萄干馅的饼皮，似乎他的

Hard Times
艰难时世 15

hair, which **bristled** on the skirts of his bald head, a plantation of firs to keep the wind from its shining surface, all covered with knobs, like the **crust** of a plum pie, as if the head had scarcely warehouse-room for the hard facts stored inside. The speaker's obstinate carriage, square coat, square legs, square shoulders, —nay, his very neckcloth, trained to take him by the throat with an unaccommodating grasp, like a **stubborn** fact, as it was, —all helped the emphasis.

"In this life, we want nothing but Facts, sir; nothing but Facts!"

脑子里面已经没有空间再来存储硬性事实。还有说话者生硬的姿态，板板整整的外衣、四四方方的大腿和四四方方的肩膀——哦，还有，他的领带像一个固执的事实，练就了抓住他的喉咙的本领——总之，这一切都加强了这种语气。

"在这一生中，我们只需要事实，先生；除了事实，什么也不需要！"

单词解析 Word Analysis

vault [vɔːlt] *n.* 拱顶

例 The vault of this cathedral is very high.
这座天主教堂的拱顶非常高。

commodious [kəˈməʊdiəs] *adj.* 宽敞的

例 Guestrooms are commodious and well-appointed.
客房宽敞舒适且陈设考究。

dictatorial [ˌdɪktəˈtɔːriəl] *adj.* 独裁的；专横傲慢的

例 I resent his dictatorial manner.
我痛恨他的独断作风。

bristle [ˈbrɪsl] *v.* 使（毛发等像鬃毛似的）直立

例 His bestiality made people bristle with anger.
他的禽兽行为令人发指。

crust [krʌst] *n.* 外壳

例 Bake until the crust is golden.

063

把糕饼烤至外皮呈金黄色。

stubborn ['stʌbən] *adj* 顽固的，固执的

例 He is an old and stubborn man.
他是个固执的老头儿。

语法知识点 Grammar Points

① **This is the principle on which I bring up my own children, and this is the principle on which I bring up these children.**

"on principle" 依据自己的原则（所确定的信念）

例 He would vote against it on principle.
他会根据原则投反对票。

② **The emphasis was helped by the speaker's square wall of a forehead, which had his eyebrows for its base, while his eyes found commodious cellarage in two dark caves, overshadowed by the wall.**

"which" 引导非限制性定语从句，代替forehead，"while"连词，表转折，起到连接的作用。"overshadowed" 为非谓语动词，表示被动，此处的逻辑关系应为 "the two dark caves are overshadowed by the wall."。

例 He is reading a book written by Bill Gates.
他在读一本比尔·盖茨写的书。

③ **The speaker's obstinate carriage, square coat, square legs, square shoulders, —nay, his very neckcloth, trained to take him by the throat with an unaccommodating grasp, like a stubborn fact, as it was, —all helped the emphasis.**

"trained" 为非谓语动词，表示被动，此处的逻辑关系应为 "his very neckcloth, trained to take him by the throat"。

"as it was" 事实上，实际上；像过去一样

例 The construction industry is no longer as depressed as it was.
建筑业不再像以往那样萧条了。

经典名句 Famous Classics

1. Youth and white paper take any impression.
   青春如白纸，最易留痕迹。

2. The dog barks in vain at the moon.
   狗对月叫，白费力气。

3. Death before dishonor.
   宁死不辱。

4. Death is common to all.
   人皆有一死。

5. A bully is always a coward.
   以强凌弱者往往是懦夫。

6. The doctor is often more to be feared than the disease.
   庸医往往比疾病更可怕。

7. One thing at a time.
   一心不能二用。

8. Opportunity, sooner or later, comes to all who work and wish
   只要努力工作而有志向，机会迟早会来临。

9. The dogs bark, but the caravan goes on.
   我行我素，岂管他哉。

读书笔记

16 Ivanhoe
艾凡赫

Many other travelers were also on their way to the town, for a great **tournament** was to be held there. Prince John, **Regent** of England in King Richard's absence, would preside. The winner of the tournament would be allowed to name the Queen of Love and Beauty and receive the prize of the passage of arms from her hands.

Ivanhoe attended the tournament with the word Disinherited written upon his shield. Entering the lists, he struck the shield of Bois-Guilbert with the point of his lance and challenged that knight to mortal combat. In the first passage both knights **splintered** their lances but neither was unhorsed. At the second passage Ivanhoe's lance struck Bois-Guilbert's helmet and upset him. Then one by one Ivanhoe **vanquished** five Knights who had agreed to take on all comers. When the heralds declared the Disinherited Knight victor of the tourney, Ivanhoe named Rowena the Queen of Love and Beauty.

In the tournament on the following day Ivanhoe was pressed hard by three **antagonists**, but he received unexpected

其他出行的人也在去往小镇的路上，因为那儿要举办一场大型锦标赛。理查德国王不出席，这次锦标赛由英格兰摄政王约翰王子主持。锦标赛的获胜者有权决定哪一名女子成为"爱与美的女王"，并由她亲手给获胜者颁发奖品。

艾凡赫穿着写有"丧失继承权"字样的盔甲加入了锦标赛。一加入竞技场，艾凡赫就用长矛刺向博伊斯·吉尔伯特的盔甲，向这位骑士发出殊死搏斗的挑战。在第一场战斗中，两位骑士的长矛都被双方击碎了，但谁也没有从马上摔落。第二场中艾凡赫的矛击中了博伊斯·吉尔伯特的头盔，把他掀翻在地。随后，艾凡赫又战胜了五个骑士，他们之前约定好要对付所有人。在信使通报"丧失继承权的骑士"为马背上比武的胜利者后，艾凡赫给爱与美的女王取名为洛伊娜。

在第二天的锦标赛中，艾凡赫被三个对手紧紧压迫着，但是他意外地得到了一位身穿黑色衣服骑士的帮助，由于此

help from a knight in black, whom the spectators had called the Black Sluggard because of his previous inactivity. Ivanhoe, because of his earlier triumphs during the day, was named champion of the tournament once more. In order to receive the gift from Lady Rowena, Ivanhoe had to remove his helmet. When he did so, he was recognized. He received the **chaplet**, his prize, kissed the hand of Lady Rowena, and then fainted from loss of blood. Isaac of York and his daughter, Rebecca, were sitting nearby, and Rebecca suggested to her father that they nurse Ivanhoe until he was well. Isaac and his daughter started for their home with the wounded knight carried in a horse litter. On the way they joined the train of Cedric the Saxon, who was still ignorant of the Disinherited Knight's identity.

前表现并不活跃，观众称他为"黑衣懒汉"。艾凡赫前一天取得了一次胜利，今天又一次被大家称为冠军。为了接收洛伊娜夫人的礼物，艾凡赫必须摘掉头盔。当他摘掉头盔时，他得到了表彰。他得到了那个作为奖品的花冠，吻了洛伊娜女士的手之后，他由于失血过多逐渐失去了意识。约克的艾萨克和他的女儿丽贝卡当时就坐在附近，丽贝卡向父亲提议由他们照顾艾凡赫直到他好起来。艾萨克和女儿出发准备回家，他们把这位受伤的骑士和一窝马的幼崽放在一起运回去。路上他们加入撒克逊人塞德里克一行人，而塞德里克仍不知道他就是"丧失继承权的骑士"。

单词解析 Word Analysis

tournament ['tʊənəmənt] *n.* 锦标赛，联赛；中世纪的骑士比武

例 She had been videoing the highlights of the tournament.
她一直在制作锦标赛集锦的录像。

regent ['riːdʒənt] *n.* 摄政者

例 The regent carried out an advanced system in his country.
摄政者在他的国家推行了一套先进的制度。

splinter ['splɪntə(r)] *v.* （使）分裂，（使）碎裂

我的名著美文：人不是生来就要被打败的

例 The mirror cracked but did not splinter.
镜子裂了，但没碎。

vanquish ['væŋkwɪʃ] v. (文)征服；战胜

例 He tried to vanquish his fears.
他努力克服恐惧心理。

antagonist [æn'tægənɪst] n. 敌手

例 His antagonist in the debate was quicker than him.
在辩论中他的对手比他反应快。

chaplet ['tʃæplət] n. 花冠

例 It is a chaplet with gold or jewels.
这是一个镶有金子和珠宝的花环。

语法知识点 Grammar Points

① **Prince John, Regent of England in King Richard's absence, would preside.**

Regent of England 作 Prince John 的同位语。
"in one's absence" 在某人不在的时候

例 She will act for the headmaster in his absence.
校长外出期间将由她代理。

② **The winner of the tournament would be allowed to name the Queen of Love and Beauty and receive the prize of the passage of arms from her hands.**

"passage" 通过，经过，"tournament" 中世纪的骑士比武
"be allowed to do" 被允许做……

例 I was allowed to do whatever I wanted with my life.
我可以自由支配自己的生活。

③ **Entering the lists, he struck the shield of Bois-Guilbert with the point of his lance and challenged that knight to mortal combat.**

"entering the lists" 是独立结构，表示"……，就……"。
"challenge sb. to mortal combat" 与……展开殊死搏斗

④ **In the tournament on the following day Ivanhoe was pressed hard by three antagonists, but he received unexpected help from a knight in black, whom the spectators had called the Black Sluggard because of his previous inactivity.**

"whom"引导非限制性定语从句，指代a knight in black，在后半句中作宾语，相当于"the spectators had called a knight in black the Black Sluggard"。

"in +颜色"穿……颜色服饰

⑤ **On the way they joined the train of Cedric the Saxon, who was still ignorant of the Disinherited Knight's identity.**

"who"引导非限制性定语从句，指代Cedric the Saxon。

"train"在此句中译为"行列"

"be ignorant of"不知道……，对……一无所知

例 Many people are worryingly ignorant of the facts about global warming.
许多人竟然不知道地球变暖的事实，实在令人担忧。

经典名句 Famous Classics

1. Death pays all debts.
   一死百债清。

2. Deeds, not words.
   要行动，不要空谈。

3. Delays are not denials.
   拖延并不是拒绝。

4. The dog that has been beaten with a stick is afraid of its shadow.
   狗儿被棒打，见到棒影就怕。（一朝被蛇咬，十年怕井绳。）

5. The dog that minds not your whistle is good for nothing.
   不听指挥的狗，一无是处。

6. Your purse opened not when it was paid for.
   不是自己买的东西就不珍惜。

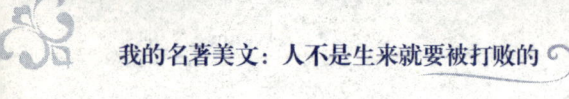

9. A busy man is plagued with one desire, but an idle one with a thousand.
忙人为一个欲望而苦恼，闲人被无数欲望所折磨。

10. Dexterity comes by experience.
熟练来自经验。

11. The devil never sleeps.
魔鬼从不休息。（要时时小心，以免灾祸上身。）

读书笔记

17 Jane Eyre
简·爱

My first quarter at Lowood seemed an age; and not the golden age either; it comprised an **irksome** struggle with difficulties in habituating myself to new rules and **unwonted** tasks. The fear of failure in these points **harassed** me worse than the physical hardships of my lot; though these were no trifles.

During January, February, and part of March, the deep snows, and, after their melting, the almost **impassable** roads, prevented our stirring beyond the garden walls, except to go to church; but within these limits we had to pass an hour every day in the open air. Our clothing was insufficient to protect us from the severe cold: we had no boots, the snow got into our shoes and melted there: our ungloved hands became numbed and covered with **chilblains**, as were our feet: I remember well the distracting irritation I endured from this cause every evening, when my feet **inflamed**; and the torture of thrusting the swelled, raw, and stiff toes into my shoes in the morning. Then the scanty supply of food was distressing: with the keen appetites of growing children, we had scarcely sufficient to keep alive a

我在罗沃德的一个季度似乎有一个时代那么长，而且还不是黄金时代；为了适应新规则和不熟悉的工作就需要同种种令人厌恶的困难作斗争。虽说艰苦也并不是小事，但相比之下，我更加担心在这方面出什么差错。

一月、二月和三月的几天里，大雪纷飞，厚厚的雪消融之后，几乎阻断了我们花园外所有的路，除了去教堂的路。但是在这些限制条件下，我们每天都要在户外度过一个小时。我们的衣服不足以御寒：我们没有靴子，雪进入我们的鞋子，就在里面融化，我们赤裸的双手变得麻木，长满冻疮，我们的脚也是如此：我清楚地记得，每天夜里，当我的脚肿起来的时候，我心烦意乱；清晨，把又肿又僵的脚趾放进鞋里的折磨，让人难以忍受。那时，令人苦恼的是食物供应不足：正在成长的孩子的食欲非常好，但我们所得到的却不足以养活一个脆弱的病人。食物不足导致了虐待，对

delicate invalid. From this deficiency of **nourishment** resulted an abuse, which pressed hardly on the younger pupils: whenever the **famished** great girls had an opportunity, they would coax or **menace** the little ones out of their portion. Many a time I have shared between two claimants the precious morsel of brown bread distributed at teatime; and after **relinquishing** to a third half the contents of my mug of coffee, I have swallowed the **remainder** with an accompaniment of secret tears, forced from me by the **exigency** of hunger.

年幼的学生的影响最为严重。每当饿坏了的略大一些的女孩逮到机会，她们就会哄骗甚至是威胁小一点儿的女孩交出自己分得的食物。很多时候，我和另外两个索要者分享在下午茶时间分得的珍贵的小块儿棕色面包。在第三次被迫交出一半咖啡后，迫于极度饥饿，我强迫自己把剩下的都吞了下去，一起吞下去的还有我默默流下的泪水。

单词解析 Word Analysis

irksome ['ə:ksəm] *adj.* 令人烦恼的；惹人生气的

例　It is irksome to listen to his constant complaints.
　　他无休止的抱怨真让人心烦。

unwonted [ˌʌn'wəntid, ʌn'wʌn-] *adj.* 不寻常的；不平常的

例　He spoke with unwonted enthusiasm.
　　他讲话显得出人意料地热心。

harass ['hærəs] *v.* 侵扰，骚扰；不断攻击

例　He has complained of being harassed by the police.
　　他投诉自己受到了警察的侵扰。

impassable [im'pɑ:səbl] *adj.* 不能通行的

例　The mud made the road impassable.
　　由于淤泥道路无法通行。

chilblain ['tʃilblein] *n.* 冻疮

例 The soles of his feet were raw with chilblain.
他脚底长的冻疮很疼。

inflame [in'fleim] *v.* （使）发怒
例 His comments flamed all the people all around China.
他的言论激怒了全中国的人。

nourishment ['nʌriʃmənt] *n.* 食物；营养
例 He was unable to take nourishment for several days.
他已经有好几天没能吃东西了。

famished ['fæmiʃt] *adj.* 挨饿的
例 Before each competition, he spends most of a month famished.
每次赛前的一个月里，他基本上都在挨饿。

menace ['menəs] *v.* 威胁；恐吓
例 The big hole outside the house is a menace to children's safety.
房外的大洞对孩子的安全是个威胁。

relinquish [ri'liŋkwiʃ] *v.* （尤指不情愿地）放弃
例 He was forced to relinquish control of the company.
他被迫放弃公司的控制权。

remainder [ri'meində(r)] *n.* 剩余物
例 I kept some of his books and gave away the remainder.
我保留了他的一些书，其余的送人了。

exigency ['eksidʒənsi] *n.* 紧急需要，迫切需要
例 The president is free to act in any sudden exigency.
出现任何突发的紧急状况，董事长可以自行采取行动。

语法知识点 Grammar Points

① **It comprised an irksome struggle with difficulties in habituating myself to new rules and unwonted tasks.**

"the struggle with/against" 为 "和……作斗争" 之意。

例 He struggled with her conscience before talking to the police.
他和警察交谈前作了一番良心上的斗争。

"habituate oneself to..." 适应、习惯于……

例 You must habituate yourself to hard work.
你必须习惯艰苦的工作。

② **Our clothing was insufficient to protect us from the severe cold: we had no boots, the snow got into our shoes and melted there.**

"be insufficient to" 不足以……，不够……

例 His salary is insufficient to meet his needs.
他的薪水不能满足他的需求。

③ **Whenever the famished great girls had an opportunity, they would coax or menace the little ones out of their portion.**

"whenever" 引导让步状语从句，表示"无论什么时候，不管什么时候"，此句中涉及了时态配合：从句为一般过去时，主句为过去将来时，表示一种过去时常发生的事件。

例 Whenever she refused, he would beat her black and blue.
只要她拒绝就会被他打得青一块紫一块的。

经典名句 Famous Classics

1. The dog that trots about finds a bone.
   勤于跑的狗才有骨头啃。

2. The eagle does not catch flies.
   办大事者不拘小节。

3. Deliberate slowly, execute promptly.
   慢慢酌量，快快行动。

4. Depend on others and you always repent.
   依靠别人总要后悔。

5. Pigs see the wind.
   猪烦躁，风暴到。

6. The chief disease that reigns this year is folly.
当今最流行的疾病就是愚蠢。

7. One thing thinks the horse, and another he that saddles.
各有各的想法。（仁者见仁，智者见智。）

读书笔记

18 Jude the Obscure
无名的裘德

Deprived of the objects of both intellect and emotion, he could not proceed to his work. Whenever he felt reconciled to his fate as a student, there came to disturb his calm his hopeless relations with Sue. That the one **affined** soul he had ever met was lost to him through his marriage returned upon him with cruel persistency, till, unable to bear it longer, he again rushed for distraction to the real Christminster life. He now sought it out in an obscure and low-ceiled tavern up a court which was well known to certain worthies of the place, and in brighter times would have interested him simply by its **quaintness**. Here he sat more or less all the day, convinced that he was at bottom a vicious character, of whom it was hopeless to expect anything.

In the evening the frequenters of the house dropped in one by one, Jude still retaining his seat in the corner, though his money was all spent, and he had not eaten anything the whole day except a biscuit. He surveyed his gathering companions with all the **equanimity** and philosophy of a man who has been drinking long and

他既不能够追求学问又得不到爱情,也就没心情再去继续干活了。每当他自认命中注定当不上大学生,心境逐渐平静下来时候,他跟苏之间渺无希望的关系就来搅扰他。他这辈子遇上的人中,只有苏和他意气相投,可由于他结过婚,就不可能同苏结婚,这件事一直残酷地萦绕在他心头,逼得他没法忍受。他心烦意乱,只好一头奔出去,寻找那真正的基督徒生活来分散注意力。于是,他来到一个坐落在大院子上边的一家偏僻的矮屋顶小酒馆,当地的一些名流也光顾那地方。要是在他平时心情比较畅快的时候,他会觉得那离奇古怪的模样很是有趣,不过这会儿就不然了。他在那儿一坐差不多一整天,认定自己生性堕落,不能指望自己有所作为。

傍晚时分,小酒馆的常客陆续光临了。尽管他的钱已经花光了,裘德还是坐在屋角的座位上,他这一整天只吃了块饼干。他一直坐在那慢慢地喝酒,沉着冷静地观察着周围的人,还和其中的几个交上了

slowly, and made friends with several: to wit, Tinker Taylor, a decayed church-ironmonger who appeared to have been of a religious turn in earlier years, but was somewhat **blasphemous** now; also a red-nosed auctioneer; also two Gothic masons like himself, called Uncle Jim and Uncle Joe. There were present, too, some clerks, and a gown-and surplice-maker's assistant; two ladies who sported moral characters of various depths of shade, according to their company, nicknamed "Bower o' Bliss"and "Freckles"; some horsey men "in the know"of betting circles; a travelling actor from the theatre, and two **devil-may-care** young men who proved to be gownless undergraduates; they had slipped in by stealth to meet a man about bull-pups, and stayed to drink and smoke short pipes with the racing gents aforesaid, looking at their watches every now and then.

朋友：一个是廷克·泰勒，他原先专做教堂五金生意，那会儿信教信得挺虔诚，这会儿对教会也有了不敬的言辞；一个是红鼻头拍卖商；还有两个和他一样干哥特式石雕的石匠，人称吉爷和乔爷。在座的另有几个小职员；一个牧师服饰制作商的帮工；还有两位女士，一个外号叫"安乐窝"，另一个为"麻点子"，她们的道德品味遇好则好，遇劣则劣；几个号称深谙赛马场上赌博圈的男人；一个剧院的巡回演员；两个没穿校服、怡然自得的大学生，他们偷偷溜进了酒馆来见一个人，商量几只小公狗的事。他们待在那儿和前面提到的赌赛马的绅士们在一块儿喝酒，拿短烟管抽烟，不时还看看表。

单词解析 Word Analysis

deprive [dɪˈpraɪv] v. 剥夺，夺去，使丧失

例 To deprive the boy of his education is a violation of state law.
剥夺这个男孩受教育的权利是一种违反国家法律的行为。

affined [əˈfaɪnd] adj. 受约束的，有密切关系的

例 However now, he has been formed with Baoermo open and affined.
然而现在，他已经和鲍尔默结成公开同盟。

我的名著美文：人不是生来就要被打败的

quaintness [kweɪntnəs] *n.* 离奇有趣，古怪的事物

例 Some words in her dialect had a charming quaintness.
她说过的带有方言的一些话中有种可爱的意趣。

equanimity [ˌekwəˈnɪməti] *n.* 平和，镇静

例 She accepted the prospect of her operation with equanimity.
她心情平静地接受了动手术的可能性。

blasphemous [ˈblæsfəməs] *adj.* 亵渎上帝的，亵渎宗教信仰的

例 She was accused of being blasphemous.
她被控亵渎神明。

devil-may-care *adj.* 不顾一切的，漫不经心的

例 I love Italian food and wine and the devil-may-care attitude of the people.
我喜欢意大利的食物、美酒和人们那种天塌下来当被盖的心态。

语法知识点 Grammar Points

① **Deprived of the objects of both intellect and emotion, he could not proceed to his work.**

"be deprived of" 被剥夺，被夺去

例 She was deprived of schooling at ten.
她10岁时就失学了。

② **Here he sat more or less all the day, convinced that he was at bottom a vicious character, of whom it was hopeless to expect anything.**

"more or less" 差不多，几乎；大约

例 I've more or less finished the book.
我差不多已经读完这本书了。

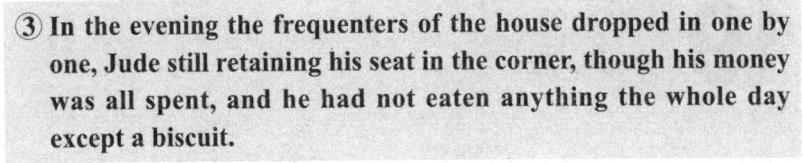

③ **In the evening the frequenters of the house dropped in one by one, Jude still retaining his seat in the corner, though his money was all spent, and he had not eaten anything the whole day except a biscuit.**

"drop in" 顺便拜访；投入

例 Whenever I'm up there I always drop in.
每次我到那儿都会顺便去看看。

经典名句 Famous Classics

1. Desire has no rest.
   欲望无止境。

2. The darkest place is under the candlestick.
   蜡烛架下最黑暗。（蜡烛照人不照己。）

3. Diet cures more than doctors.
   自己饮食有节，胜过上门求医。

4. The devil rebukes sin.
   贼喊捉贼。

5. The die is cast.
   事已成定局，不可改变。

6. Oppression makes a wise man mad.
   人处压迫下，聪明也会疯。

7. People are more convinced by words than by blows.
   言语比棍棒更能说服人。

8. One shoe will not fit all feet.
   一鞋难适众足。（不能以一种尺度衡量一切。）

19 Love of Life
热爱生命

Now and again the wolves, in packs of two and three, crossed his path. But they sheered clear of him. They were not in sufficient numbers, and besides they were hunting the **caribou**, which did not battle, while this strange creature that walked **erect** might scratch and bite.

In the late afternoon he came upon scattered bones where the wolves had made a kill. What remained had been a young caribou an hour before. He studied the bones, cleaned of any flesh. They were still pink with the life in them which had not yet died. Might he look like that before the day was done? Was this life? A fleeting thing without meaning? It was only life that pained. There was no hurt in death. To die was to sleep. It meant rest. Then why was he not content to die?

But he did not think about these things for very long. He was soon seated in the grass, a bone in his mouth, biting at the bit of life that made it yet pink. The sweet meaty taste drove him mad. He closed his teeth firmly on the bones. Sometimes it was the bone that broke, sometimes his teeth. Then he

那些狼偶尔三三两两在他面前走过，但都避开了他。原因主要有两点：其一是因为它们数量不足，其二是它们在狩猎驯鹿。驯鹿不能搏斗，而眼前这个奇怪的生物直立行走，还有可能会抓会咬。

傍晚时分，他看到散落一地的骨头，这说明狼曾在这儿猎食。一个小时前，这些骨头还是一只小驯鹿。他研究这些被咬得锃亮的骨头。还没有死去的细胞泛着粉红色。天黑前他也会变成这样吗？这就是生命吗？一件匆匆而过又毫无意义的事儿？只有活着才能感到痛苦。死了也就没什么伤害了。死亡就是睡觉，意味着休息。那么，人为什么不甘心死去呢？

但是，他对这些事情想得不长。他很快就坐在了草丛中，嘴里叼着一块骨头，咬向象征着生命的粉色处。甜甜的肉味使他疯狂。他紧紧咬住骨头。有时他咬碎的是一点儿骨头，有时他咬碎的是他的牙齿。他用岩石把骨头打碎成一

Love of Life 热爱生命 19

crushed the bones between the rocks. He pounded them into tiny pieces, and ate them. He was in such a hurry that he **pounded** his fingers, too. He felt surprised at the fact that his fingers did not hurt much when they were caught under the rock.

Then came **frightful** days of snow and rain. He did not know when he made camp and when he broke camp. He traveled in the night as much as in the day. He rested whenever he fell, moving ahead whenever the dying life in him started up again. He, as a man, no longer struggled. It was the life in him, unwilling to die, that drove him on. He did not suffer, nor feel pain. But his mind was filled with **hallucinations** and wild dreams.

个个小块，再吃掉它们。由于他很着急，有时也会砸到自己的手指。令他吃惊的是，当他手指碰巧被石头打到也不怎么疼。

接着下了几天可怕的雨和雪。他不知道什么时候露营，什么时候结束。他在夜里走的路和白天一样多。他在哪里摔倒就在哪里休息，当他毫无生气的生命重拾生气时他就继续前进。他不再像人类那样挣扎了。逼着他前行的是他的生命，因为他不想死。他既不受折磨也感受不到痛苦。但他的脑海中充满了各种幻象和荒诞的梦境。

单词解析 Word Analysis

caribou ['kærɪbuː] *n.* （北美洲产的）驯鹿

例 Afar off he heard the squawking of caribou calves.
他听到远处有一群小驯鹿尖叫的声音。

erect [ɪ'rekt] *adj.* 直立的，垂直的

例 Stand with your arms by your side and your head erect.
手放两边，昂首站立。

pound [paʊnd] *v.* 连续重击，咚咚地走

例 Someone was pounding at the door.
有人在砰砰地敲门。

081

我的名著美文：人不是生来就要被打败的

frightful ['fraɪtfl] *adj.* 可怕的；惊人的

例 The battle resulted in a frightful slaughter.
战斗以可怕的大屠杀告终。

hallucination [həˌluːsɪ'neɪʃn] *n.* 幻觉，幻想；错觉

例 High temperatures can cause hallucination.
高烧可使人产生幻觉。

语法知识点 Grammar Points

① **Now and again the wolves, in packs of two and three, crossed his path.**

"now and again" 时而，偶尔，有时

例 I earn enough to push the boat out now and again.
我挣的钱足以时不时摆摆阔了。

② **He was soon seated in the grass, a bone in his mouth, biting at the bit of life that made it yet pink.**

"a bone in his mouth" 作插入语，"biting" 是非谓语动词。

③ **He was in such a hurry that he pounded his fingers, too.**

"in a hurry" 立刻；迅速地

例 Dave was in a hurry to get back to work.
戴夫急于回到工作岗位。

④ **He rested whenever he fell, moving ahead whenever the dying life in him started up again.**

"whenever" 引导时间状语从句，无论什么时候，只要……的时候。
"moving" 作伴随状语
"start up" 开始，着手

例 I heard his car start up.
我听见他的汽车发动了。

⑤ **It was the life in him, unwilling to die, that drove him on.**

句子的主干是：It was the life in him that drove him on.

082

it is/was...that...为一个强调句
"unwilling" 作伴随状语，表示状态。

经典名句 Famous Classics

1. The cow does not make the monk.
   穿袈裟的不一定是和尚。（人不可貌相。）

2. The dainties of the great are the tears of the poor.
   富人口中的美味是穷人的眼泪。

3. The danger past and God forgotten.
   度过了危险，就忘了上帝。（好了伤疤，就忘了痛。）

4. Diligence brings about fruitful results.
   勤劳出硕果。

5. Diligence is near success.
   勤奋近乎成功。

6. The darkest hour is that before the dawn.
   黎明之前最黑暗。

7. The day is short but the work is much.
   工作多，时光迫。

8. Other times, other manners.
   时代不同，风俗有异。（俗随时变。）

9. A bleating sheep loses a bite.
   说话太多，错失良机。

20 Lucky Jim
幸运的吉姆

Just as they drew level with the shop-window, the door opened and a crowd of Welches came out and blocked the pavement. One of them was clearly the **effeminate** writing Michel, on stage at last just as the curtain was about to ring down. He was a tall pale young man with long pale hair protruding from under a pale corduroy cap. Sensing the approach of passers-by, the whole group, with the natural exception of Welch himself, began automatically shifting about out of the way. Dixon squeezed Christine's arm encouragingly and walked up to them. "Excuse me," he said in a **fruity** comic-butler voice.

On Mrs. Welch's face appeared an expression of imminent vomiting; Dixon inclined his head indulgently to her. (He remembered something in a book about success making people humble, tolerant, and kind.)The incident was almost closed when he saw that not only were Welch and Bertrand both present, but Welch's fishing-hat and Bertrand's **beret** were there too. The beret, however, was on Welch's head, the fishing-hat on Bertrand's. In these **guises**, and standing

正当他们走到商店橱窗前时，门突然开了，威尔奇家的人走了出来，堵住了人行道。其中有一人显然是阴柔气息十足的米歇尔，他在即将落幕时出现在舞台上。他是一个身材高大、脸色苍白的年轻人，他白色的头发从白白的灯芯绒帽子下伸展出来。感觉到越来越近的行人，整个团队，自然韦尔奇本人除外，开始自动让路。狄克逊鼓足勇气紧抓着克里斯汀的手臂，向他们走去，"借过。"他用一种像管家一样圆润的声音说道。

威尔奇太太的脸上呈现出马上要呕吐的表情；狄克逊宽容地向她点了点头（他记得一本书中写着成功让人谦虚、宽容和友善）。就在这个小插曲快要结束时，他看到在场的不仅有威尔奇和贝特朗，还有威尔奇的钓鱼帽和贝特朗的贝雷帽。只不过，贝雷帽戴在了威尔奇的头上，钓鱼帽在贝特朗的头上。他们这样打扮，僵硬地站在那儿，眼睛还叽里咕噜地直转，像出自学徒之手的吉

rigid with popping eyes, as both were, they had a look of being Gide and Lytton Strachey, represented in waxwork form by a prentice hand. Dixon drew in breath to **denounce** them both, then blew it all out again in a howl of laughter. His steps faltered; his body sagged as if he'd been knifed. With Christine **tugging** at his arm he halted in the middle of the group, slowly doubling up like a man with the stitch, his spectacles misting over with the exertion of it, his mouth stuck **ajar** in a rictus of agony."You're..."he said. "He's..."

The Welches withdrew and began getting into their car. Moaning, Dixon allowed Christine to lead him away up the street. The whinnying and clanging of Welch's self-starter began behind them, growing fainter and fainter as they walked on until it was altogether overlaid by the other noises of the town and by their own voices.

德和利顿·斯克奇的蜡像。狄克逊吸了口气准备痛斥这二人，然而他又把气全都吐了出来变为一阵狂笑。他脚步不稳、身体下垂，好像被刀砍了一样。当克里丝汀拖着他的胳膊在这些人中停了下来时，他笑得慢慢弯下了腰，像用线连接着一样，眼镜在笑声中起了薄薄的一层雾，他的嘴巴微张，因痛苦而咧着嘴 "你是……"他说，"他是……"

威尔奇一家离开，进到车里。狄克逊呻吟着，任由克里斯汀带着他沿街走去。威尔奇开始在他们身后发出各种嘶嘶声和叮当声，随着他们越走越远，声音也越来越弱，最后掩埋在其他噪声和他们的交谈声中。

单词解析 Word Analysis

effeminate [ɪˈfemɪnət] *adj* （指男人）柔弱的，女人气的

例 Also, he had effeminate voice and faces too.
同时，他也表现出了妩媚的嗓音和表情。

fruity [ˈfruːti] *adj* 圆润的

例 He laughed again, a solid, fruity laugh.
他又笑了，声音浑厚而圆润。

我的名著美文：人不是生来就要被打败的

beret [ˈbereɪ] *n.* 贝雷帽

例 He is an eccentric character who likes wearing a beret and dark glasses.
他人很怪，喜欢戴贝雷帽和墨镜。

guise [ɡaɪz] *n.* 装束；伪装

例 The story appears in different guises in different cultures.
这个故事以不同的形式出现在不同的文化中。

denounce [dɪˈnaʊns] *v.* 公开指责

例 The project was denounced as a scandalous waste of public money.
这项工程被斥责为挥霍公款，令人愤慨。

tug [tʌɡ] *v.* 用力拉，使劲拉

例 She knows exactly how to tug at readers' heartstrings.
她对如何牵动读者的心弦了如指掌。

ajar [əˈdʒɑː(r)] *adv.* 微开着

例 I'll leave the door ajar.
我让门半开着。

语法知识点 Grammar Points

① Just as they drew level with the shop-window, the door opened and a crowd of Welches came out and blocked the pavement.

"draw level (with)" 拉平（相齐）

例 The two ships draw level.
这两条船并排行驶。

"a crowd of" 很多的；一大群（人）

例 Police waded into a crowd of protesters.
警察介入，企图驱散抗议人群。

② **On Mrs Welch's face appeared an expression of imminent vomiting; Dixon inclined his head indulgently to her.**

地点状语提前，后面的句子完全倒装。正常的语序为"An expression of imminent vomiting on Mrs Welch's face"。

例 On the wall hangs a beautiful picture.
墙上挂着一幅美丽的画。

③ **Dixon drew in breath to denounce them both, then blew it all out again in a howl of laughter.**

"draw in breath" 吸气

例 Draw in a deep breath and let it out slowly.
深吸一口气，再慢慢把它呼出来。

"blow out" 吹出……

例 As a kid, I couldn't wait to blow out the candles and open gifts from my friends and family.
当我还是小孩子的时候，我迫不及待地吹灭蜡烛，急切地打开朋友和家人所送的礼物。

"a howl of" 嚎叫，一阵……的嚎叫声

例 With a howl of rage, he grabbed the neck of a broken bottle and advanced.
他一声怒吼，抓起一个破瓶子的瓶颈冲上前来。

经典名句 Famous Classics

1. Diligence redeems stupidity.
   勤能补拙。

2. Discontent is the first step in progress.
   不满足是前进的第一步。

3. The dead don't bite.
   死人泄露不了秘密。

4. The death of wolves is the safety of the sheep.
   群狼一死则众羊安。

5. A bad gardener quarrels with his rake.
   劣工咎器。

6. Pain is forgotten where gain follows.
   一朝得了利,痛苦便忘记。

7. Pardon all but thyself.
   克己恕人。

8. New kings, new laws.
   新君立新法。

9. No money, no honey.
   没有金钱,就没有爱情。

读书笔记

21 Mansfield Park
曼斯菲尔德庄园

About thirty years ago Miss Maria Ward, of Huntingdon, with only seven thousand pounds, had the good luck to **captivate** Sir Thomas Bertram, of Mansfield Park, in the county of Northampton, and to be thereby raised to the rank of a baronet's lady, with all the comforts and consequences of a handsome house and large income. All Huntingdon exclaimed on the greatness of the match, and her uncle, the lawyer, himself, allowed her to be at least three thousand pounds short of any equitable claim to it. She had two sisters to be benefited by her **elevation**; and such of their acquaintance as thought Miss Ward and Miss Frances quite as handsome as Miss Maria, did not **scruple** to predict their marrying with almost equal advantage. But there certainly are not so many men of large fortune in the world, as there are pretty women to deserve them. Miss Ward, at the end of half a dozen years, found herself obliged to be attached to the Rev. Mr. Norris, a friend of her brother-in-law, with scarcely any private fortune, and Miss Frances fared yet worse. Miss

大约三十年前，亨廷登的玛利亚·沃德小姐仅凭七千英镑的陪嫁就幸运地得到了托马斯·伯特伦爵士的倾心，托马斯·伯特伦爵士可是北安普顿郡曼斯菲尔德庄园的主人，玛利亚·沃德小姐便一举成为准男爵夫人。这样一来，她便有了漂亮的宅邸和一大笔可观的收入，过上了舒适安逸的生活。亨廷登的所有人都惊叹玛利亚小姐嫁得好，连她做律师的舅舅都说她至少得再加上三千英镑才配嫁给托马斯爵士。她攀上了这门亲事，她的两个姐妹沾了光。亲朋好友中但凡觉得沃德小姐（大女儿）和弗朗西斯小姐（小女儿）长得和玛利亚小姐一样端庄美丽的，都大胆预测她们二人会嫁得像玛利亚小姐一样好。但世界上有钱的男人没有配得上他们的女人那么多，这是肯定的。六年后，沃德小姐嫁给了她二妹夫的一个朋友——诺里斯先生，而他几乎没有什么私人财产，但弗朗西斯小姐的情况更加糟糕。托马斯爵士欣然地让

Ward's match, indeed, when it came to the point, was not **contemptible**, Sir Thomas being happily able to give his friend an income in the living of Mansfield, and Mr. and Mrs. Norris began their career of **conjugal felicity** with very little less than a thousand a year. But Miss Frances married, in the common phrase, to disoblige her family, and by fixing on a lieutenant of Marines, without education, fortune, or connections, did it very thoroughly. She could hardly have made a more untoward choice. Sir Thomas Bertram had interest, which, from principle as well as pride, from a general wish of doing right, and a desire of seeing all that were connected with him in situations of respectability, he would have been glad to exert for the advantage of Lady Bertram's sister; but her husband's profession was such as no interest could reach; and before he had time to devise any other method of assisting them, an absolute breach between the sisters had taken place. It was the natural result of the conduct of each party, and such as a very **imprudent** marriage almost always produces.

他的朋友留在曼斯菲尔德庄园里做牧师，这样一来他的朋友一年有接近一千英镑的收入，在这之后，沃德小姐的婚事确实不可悲，他们夫妻二人过上了相敬如宾的生活。可是弗朗西斯小姐的婚事呢，却是没让家里称心，应该说是让家里彻底寒心，用句俗话说，她居然看上了一没文化，二没财产，三没关系的海军陆战队中尉。这是她做过最糟糕的决定。托马斯·伯特伦爵士出于人情世故和自尊心，希望做出正确的事情，再加上他又希望和他有关联的所有人都很体面，他愿意发挥自己的力量来帮助伯特伦夫人（婚后玛利亚小姐的称呼）的妹妹。但她丈夫的这一职业中，他没有关系可以依托。还没有等他想出别的方法来帮助他们，姐妹们就彻底闹掰了。这是双方的行为必然产生的结果，大多草率的婚姻最后的结果也不外如此。

单词解析 Word Analysis

captivate ['kæptɪveɪt] *v.* 迷住，迷惑

例 The children were captivated by her stories.
孩子们被她的故事迷住了。

elevation [,elɪ'veɪʃn] *n.* 提拔；晋级；提升

例 We congratulated his elevation to the presidency.
我们对他晋升校长表示祝贺。

scruple ['skru:pl] *v.* 有顾忌

例 Don't scruple to ask for anything you want.
你要什么请尽量讲。

contemptible [kən'temptəbl] *adj.* （正）可轻蔑的，可鄙的

例 That was a contemptible trick to play on a friend.
那是对朋友玩弄的一出可鄙的把戏。

conjugal ['kɒndʒəgl] *adj.* 婚姻的，夫妻之间的

例 A couple's conjugal fate is prearranged.
缘分天定。

felicity [fə'lɪsəti] *n.* 幸福

例 Felicity is easily found, but hard to be kept.
找到幸福容易，维持幸福困难。

imprudent [ɪm'pru:dnt] *adj.* 不明智的，不谨慎的

例 It would be imprudent to invest all your money in one company.
把所有的钱都投资在一家公司是不明智的。

语法知识点 Grammar Points

① All Huntingdon exclaimed on the greatness of the match, and her uncle, the lawyer, himself, allowed her to be at least three thousand pounds short of any equitable claim to it.

"the lawyer" "himself" 都是 "her uncle" 的同位语，作后半句话的主语。

"be short of" 缺少；缺乏

例 The country is short of skilled labor.
这个国家缺乏技术娴熟的工人。

② **She had two sisters to be benefited by her elevation; and such of their acquaintance as thought Miss Ward and Miss Frances quite as handsome as Miss Maria, did not scruple to predict their marrying with almost equal advantage.**

"to be benefited" 是非谓语动词，表示将来，同时又有被动的含义。后半句句子的主干是 "such of their acquaintance did not scruple to predict their marrying with almost equal advantage"。

"marry sb./marry to/with sb." 和某人结婚

例 I think he wanted to marry her, if I am not mistaken.
我觉得他曾想娶她为妻，如果我没有弄错的话。

③ **Sir Thomas Bertram had interest, which, from principle as well as pride, from a general wish of doing right, and a desire of seeing all that were connected with him in situations of respectability, he would have been glad to exert for the advantage of Lady Bertram's sister**

前半句的主干是 "Sir Thomas Bertram had interest and a desire of..."。

"be connected with" 与……有关，与……相关

例 The police suspect this man may be connected with the incident.
警方怀疑该男子与这起事件有关。

经典名句 Famous Classics

1. True love does not come by finding the perfect person, but by learning to see an imperfect person perfectly.
获得真爱不是靠寻觅完美之人，而是学会把不完美之人看得完美。

2. It is possible to learn more of a human being in one minute of love than in months of observation.
   对一个人的了解，相恋一分钟可能胜过观察几个月。

3. If it is your time, love will track you down like a cruise missile.
   如果轮到你了，爱情会像巡航导弹一样找到你。

4. Love may be blind, but it can sure find its way around in the dark.
   爱情也许是盲目的，但它一定会在黑暗中找到路。

5. Love is not finding someone to live with. It's finding someone you can't live without.
   爱情不是找个人一块生活，而是找到那个你离不开的人。

6. Let the first impulse pass, wait for the second.
   不要理会第一次感情的冲动，等待第二次吧。

7. True love is like ghosts, which everybody talks about and few have seen.
   真正的爱情犹如幽灵，人人都谈起过，但几乎没人见过。

8. Love, while you are able to love.
   趁着能爱，尽快去爱。

读书笔记

22 Mrs. Dalloway
达洛维夫人

Far was Italy and the white houses and the room where her sisters sat making hats, and the streets crowded every evening with people walking, laughing out loud, not half alive like people here, **huddled** up in Bath chairs, looking at a few ugly flowers stuck in pots!

"For you should see the Milan gardens,"she said aloud. But to whom?

There was nobody. Her words faded. So a rocket fades. Its sparks, having **grazed** their way into the night, surrender to it, dark descends, pours over the outlines of houses and towers; **bleak** hillsides soften and fall in. But though they are gone, the night is full of them; robbed of colour, blank of windows, they exist more ponderously, give out what the frank daylight fails to transmit—the trouble and suspense of things **conglomerated** there in the darkness; huddled together in the darkness; **reft** of the relief which dawn brings when, washing the walls white and grey, spotting each window-pane, lifting the mist from the fields, showing the red-brown cows peacefully grazing,

在遥远的意大利，有白色的房子，她和姐妹们坐在一个房间里制帽，每晚街上都挤满了散步和嘻哈大笑的人，和这里半死不活的人一点也不像，她们在轮椅里缩成一团，盯着花盆中栽着的几朵丑陋的花。

"你应该去参观米兰的公园。"她大声地说着。不过是说给谁听的呀？

这里没有人。她的声音在消逝。火箭的消逝也是如此。它喷出火花冲向夜空，之后隐没在夜空中。暗夜来临，夜色笼罩着房舍和塔楼的轮廓，荒凉的山丘变得柔和了，隐没在夜色中。可是尽管它们都消失了，夜依然蕴蓄着它们；没有颜色，窗户也不见了，它们更深沉地存在着，传达出直白的白昼无法传达的意境——漆黑的夜里，事物的烦扰和悬疑聚拢在暗夜里挤成一团；夜夺去了拂晓带来的宽慰；晨晖把墙照成灰白色、照亮每扇玻璃窗、驱散田野的薄雾、展露出安静地吃着草的棕红色的奶牛，这一切又会出现在眼前，再次恢复生机。"我只身一

all is once more decked out to the eye; exists again. I am alone; I am alone! she cried, by the fountain in Regent's Park (staring at the Indian and his cross), as perhaps at midnight, when all boundaries are lost, the country reverts to its ancient shape, as the Romans saw it, lying cloudy, when they landed, and the hills had no names and rivers wound they knew not where—such was her darkness; when suddenly, as if a shelf were shot forth and she stood on it, she said how she was his wife, married years ago in Milan, his wife, and would never, never tell that he was mad! Turning, the shelf fell; down, down she dropped. For he was gone, she thought—gone, as he threatened, to kill himself—to throw himself under a cart! But no; there he was; still sitting alone on the seat, in his **shabby** overcoat, his legs crossed, staring, talking aloud.

人，我是孤独的！"她哭喊着，站在摄政公园喷泉边（盯着那印度人和他的十字架），像是在午夜，所有的边界线都消失了，国家还原成它以前的样子，就像罗马人着陆时看到的一样，万物朦胧，山峦无名，河流曲折蜿蜒不知去向——这就是她心中的黑暗。一瞬间，似乎前面冒出一块暗礁，她站上去，讲述着自己是怎样成为他的太太的，多年前与他在米兰结了婚，成了他的太太，她永远、永远都不会告诉别人他疯了！她转过身，暗礁就下沉了，她也不断地下沉、下沉……因为他离开了，她思索着——走了，和他威胁着的那样，他要去自杀——让自己死在马车下！但没有。他在那儿，他依旧一个人穿着他的破大衣在那儿坐着，他交叉着腿，瞪着眼，高声地自言自语。

单词解析 Word Analysis

huddle ['hʌdl] v. 挤在一起；蜷缩（成一团）

例 I huddled under a blanket on the floor.
我在地板上盖着毯子缩成一团。

graze [greɪz] v. 擦过，掠过

例 A bullet from one of the pistols had graze his hip.
手枪里发射出的子弹擦伤了他的臀部。

我的名著美文：人不是生来就要被打败的

bleak [bli:k] *adj.* 暗淡的，昏暗的；寒冷的

例 Her book paints a bleak picture of the problems women now face.
她的书是女性当下所面临问题的凄凉写照。

conglomerate [kənˈglɒmərət] *v.* 使聚结；使成团

例 The children conglomerated together for warmth.
孩子们挤成一团以取暖。

reave [ri:v] *v.* 剥夺，抢走

例 Proper arrangements have been made for the children who were reft of their parents.
丧失了父母的孤儿们都得到了妥善的安置。

shabby [ˈʃæbi] *adj.* 衣衫褴褛的；破旧的

例 He hesitated and told me he was brought up in a shabby and dirty town.
他吞吞吐吐地告诉我，他是在一个破旧肮脏的小镇上长大的。

语法知识点 Grammar Points

① **Far was Italy and the white houses and the room where her sisters sat making hats, and the streets crowded every evening with people walking, laughing out loud, not half alive like people here, huddled up in Bath chairs, looking at a few ugly flowers stuck in pots!**

"where"引导地点状语从句，在本句中可译为"在那个房间里"；"crowded"作"the streets"的后置定语；"walking, laughing out loud和looking at"都为非谓语动词，表示主动的动作或状态。

"be crowded with"挤满……

例 The old town square was crowded with people.
古老的小镇广场上挤满了人。

② **Its sparks, having grazed their way into the night, surrender to it, dark descends, pours over the outlines of houses and towers.**

"surrender"、"descend"分别是"投降"和"下来，降临"的意思，其动作发出者皆为人。在本句中的主语却分别为Its sparks和dark，这就涉及了拟人的修辞手法。

例 The sun looks over the mountain's rim.
太阳挂在山边。

③ **But though they are gone, the night is full of them; robbed of colour, blank of windows, they exist more ponderously, give out what the frank daylight fails to transmit—the trouble and suspense of things conglomerated there in the darkness; huddled together in the darkness**

"rob of"抢夺（某人）……

例 A last-minute goal robbed the team of victory.
最后一分钟的进球夺去了这支球队获胜的机会。

"huddle"挤在一起；缩成一团，其动作的发出者为人，所以在此也涉及了拟人的修辞手法。

④ **But no; there he was; still sitting alone on the seat, in his shabby overcoat, his legs crossed, staring, talking aloud.**

以"there, here, now, then"等引导的句子中，谓语动词常为"be, come, go"等动词，句子要完全倒装。但倘若主语是人称代词则无需倒装，如本句中的"there he was"就为正常语序。

例 Here comes the bus.
公共汽车来了。

经典名句 Famous Classics

1. Distance lends enchantment to the view.
距离产生美。

2. Do dogs not eat dog.
虎毒不食子。

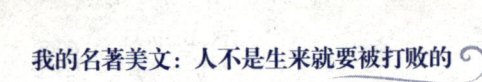

3. Do as the Romans do.
   入国问禁，入乡随俗。

4. Do as you would be done by.
   己所不欲，勿施于人。

5. The child says nothing but what it heard by the fire.
   小孩子在家里听到大人说什么，就到外面说什么。

6. The childhood shows the man, as morning shows the day.
   从童年可以看到成年，从早晨可以看到全天。（三岁看小，七岁看老。）

7. A bad excuse is better than none (at all).
   辩解总比不辩强。

8. The command of custom is great.
   习俗号召力强。

23 Oliver Twist
雾都孤儿

"Bow to the board," said Bumble. Oliver brushed away two or three tears that were lingering in his eyes, and seeing no board but the table, fortunately bowed to that.

"What's your name, boy?" said the gentleman in the high chair.

Oliver was frightened at the sight of so many gentlemen, which made him tremble: and the **beadle** gave him another tap behind, which made him cry. These two causes made him answer in a very low and hesitating voice; whereupon a gentleman in a white waistcoat said he was a fool, which was a capital way of raising his spirits, and putting him quite at his ease.

"Boy," said the gentleman in the high chair, "listen to me. You know you're an orphan, I suppose?"

"What's that, sir?" inquired poor Oliver.

"The boy is a fool--I thought he was," said the gentleman in the white waistcoat, in a very decided tone. If one member of a class be blessed with an **intuitive perception** of others of the same race, the gentleman in the white

"给各位理事鞠一躬。"邦布尔说道。奥利弗抹掉在眼里打转的两三滴泪水,他看见前面只有一张桌子,没有木板,只好将就着朝着桌子鞠了一躬。

"你叫什么名字?"坐在高椅上的绅士问道。

奥利弗一见有这么多的绅士不禁大吃一惊,浑身直哆嗦,干事又在背后捅了他一下,捅得他大哭。由于这两点原因,他回答的时候迟疑不决、声音很低。一位穿白色背心的先生当即断言奥利弗是个傻瓜。应该说明,这样做出评判是这位绅士提神舒心的一种重要方法。

"孩子,"高椅上的绅士说道,"听我说,你是个孤儿,我想你应该是知道的吧?"

"先生,那是什么?"可怜的奥利弗询问道。

"这个男孩是个傻瓜,我刚刚就说了他是个傻瓜。"穿着白色背心的绅士用非常肯定的口吻说道。如果同一阶级的成员可以体察同类人的话,毫

099

waistcoat was unquestionably well qualified to pronounce an opinion on the matter.

"Hush!"said the gentleman who had spoken first. "You know you've got no father or mother, and that you were brought up by the **parish**, don't you?"

"Yes, sir,"replied Oliver, **weeping** bitterly.

"What are you crying for?"

"I hope you say your prayers every night,"said another gentleman in a **gruff** voice. "and pray for the people who feed you, and take care of you, like a Christian.'

"Yes, sir,"**stammered** the boy. The gentleman who spoke last was unconsciously right. It would have been very like a Christian, and a marvelously good Christian too, if Oliver had prayed for the people who fed and took care of him. But he hadn't, because nobody had taught him.

"Well! You have come here to be educated, and taught a useful trade,"said the red-faced gentleman in the high chair.

"So you'll begin to pick oakum tomorrow morning at six o'clock,"added the sully one in the white waistcoat.

For the combination of both these blessings in the one simple process of picking oakum, Oliver bowed low by

无疑问，穿白色背心的绅士有资格就这个问题发声。

"嘘！"第一个说话的绅士说道。"你没有父亲也没有母亲，是被教区的人抚养长大的，这你是知道的吧？"

"是的，先生。"奥利弗边回答着边伤心地流着泪。

"你在哭什么？"

"我希望你每晚都祈祷，"另一个绅士粗暴地说道，"像基督教徒一样为那些给你提供食物和照顾你的人祈祷。"

"是的，先生。"男孩结结巴巴地回答着。其实后说话的绅士说得对——如果奥利弗为给他提供食物和照顾他的人祈祷，他就会非常像一位基督教徒，像一位极好的基督教徒。但是奥利弗并没有这样做过，因为没有人教过他。

"行了，你到这儿来是为了接受教育，是来学一门有用的手艺的。"高椅上那位红脸绅士说。

"那么，明天早上6点钟开始拆旧麻绳。"身着白色背心的暴躁绅士补充着。

为了答谢他们通过拆旧麻绳这么一个简简单单的工序，把授业和传艺这两大善举融为一体，奥利弗在干事的指导下又深深地鞠了一躬，便被匆匆忙忙

the direction of the beadle, and was then hurried away to a large ward; where, on a rough, hard bed, he **sobbed** himself to sleep. What a novel illustration of the tender laws of England! They let the **paupers** go to sleep!

地带进一间大收容室。在那里有一张又糙又硬的床，他抽抽搭搭地睡着了。它展现出了这个受人敬爱的国家的法律是多么高贵又温柔啊！他们还允许穷人睡觉呢！

单词解析 Word Analysis

beadle ['biːdəl] *n.* （旧时教区的）执事，牧师助手

例 The grim beadle now made a gesture with his staff.
狱吏此时用权杖做了个姿势。

intuitive [in'tju(ː)itiv] *adj.* 有直觉力的；凭直觉获知的

例 He had an intuitive sense of what the reader wanted.
他有感受到读者需要什么的知觉。

perception [pə'sepʃən] *n.* 感觉；知觉

例 She showed great perception in her assessment of the family situation.
她对家庭状况的分析显示出敏锐的洞察力。

parish ['pæriʃ] *n.* （尤指英国圣公会和罗马天主教会由一个牧师管理并有一个主教堂的）教区

例 A parish is a village or part of a town which has its own church and priest.
教区有自己的教堂牧师，通常是一座小村庄或小城的一部分。

weep [wiːp] *v.* （通常因悲伤）哭泣

例 I could have wept thinking about what I'd missed.
想到失去的东西，我真的想大哭一场。

gruff [grʌf] *adj.* 粗声粗气的

例 His gruff exterior concealed one of the kindest hearts.
他粗暴的外表下藏着一颗非常善良的心。

stammer ['stæmə] v. 口吃地说

例 She was barely able to stammer out a description of her attacker.
她只能勉强结结巴巴描述一下袭击她的人。

sob [sɔb] v. 啜泣，呜咽，抽噎

例 He sobbed out his troubles.
他哭着说出了自己的烦恼。

pauper ['pɔ:pə] n. 穷人

例 Legend has it that the fairy princess fell in love with a pauper.
相传，那位仙女般的公主爱上了一个穷小子。

语法知识点 Grammar Points

① Bow to the board.

board 在本文中是双关的修辞手法，其双重语义为：（1）木板；（2）委员会，董事会。其实邦布尔指的是委员会，而奥利弗没有听懂，理解成了木板。这在下文中的"seeing no board but the table"有暗示。侧面反映出了奥利弗的内心活动以及当时所处的窘境。

② Oliver brushed away two or three...fortunately bowed to that.

词组brush away意思是把（某物）扫掉，刷掉。

例 He shook his head slightly to brush away the memories.
他轻轻地摇了摇头，驱散了往事的回忆。

此句较长，涉及一个定语从句和伴随状语从句。that引导出限制性定语从句且代替主语two or three tears。而seeing no board作伴随状语，表示主语的动作，其实动作的发出者为Oliver。

例 He sat in the armchair, reading a newspaper.
他坐在扶手椅里读报。

③ If one member of a class blessed with an intuitive perception of others of the same race...an opinion on the matter.

该句运用了反语的修辞手法。词组be blessed with是被赋予，享有……的意思。

例 She's blessed with excellent health.
她身体很好，是一种福气。

be qualified to do 有资格做……

例 I don't know much about it, so I don't feel qualified to comment.
关于此事我所知不多，所以觉得没资格评论。

pronounce是"发声"的意思。pronounce an opinion指个人想法说出来，有讽刺的意味（对比express an opinion）。

整句话的言外之意为：穿白色背心的绅士和奥利弗生存于不同的社会阶层，他不可能体察奥利弗，也没有资格随意发表言论。

④ **The gentleman who spoke last was unconsciously right.**

此句中涉及矛盾修辞法（Oxymoron）。right是正确的意思，在评判一件事正确与否的时候一定是有意识的，而用无意识意思的unconsciously修饰right，就形成了矛盾修辞。

类似的用法还有：

orderly chaos 又乱又整齐、the living death 行尸走肉、victorious defeat 虽败犹荣、an old young man 老成的年轻人。

⑤ **What a noble illustration of the tender laws of this favoured country! They let the paupers go to sleep!**

此处也为讽刺。第一句话为感叹句，句型为：what a/an/the +可数名词单数+ it is! 此句省略了it is。此句型的感叹句用法：What a fine day it is!
What引导的感叹句拓展：What+形容词+可数名词复数+主语+谓语动词！

例 What good teachers they are!
他们是多么好的老师啊！

What+形容词+不可数名词+主语+谓语（动词）！

例 What thick ice we are having here!
我们这儿的冰多厚啊！

睡觉本是人人都享有的权利，用法律允许穷人睡觉来体现法律对于穷人的残忍，同时也与noble, tender形成鲜明对比。

我的名著美文：人不是生来就要被打败的

经典名句 *Famous Classics*

1. A little learning is a dangerous thing.
   一知半解，危害不浅。

2. To err is human.
   人非圣贤孰能无过。

3. Rome is not built in a day.
   冰冻三尺非一日之寒。

4. If you give a man a fish, you feed him for a day; but if you teach him how to fish, you feed him for life.
   授人以鱼不如授人以渔。

5. Nothing venture, nothing have.
   不入虎穴焉得虎子。

6. The wit of three cobblers combined surpasses that of Zhuge Liang's.
   三个臭皮匠顶个诸葛亮。

7. It's better to do well than to say well.
   说得好不如做得好。

读书笔记

24 On Love
论爱情

The stage is more **beholding** to love, than the life of man. For as to the stage, love is ever matter of comedies, and now and then of tragedies; but in life it doth much mischief; sometimes like a **siren**, sometimes like a **fury**.

You may observe, that amongst all the great and worthy persons (whereof the memory remained, either ancient or recent) there is not one, that has been transported to the mad degree of love: which shows that great spirits, and great business, do keep out this weak passion. You must except, nevertheless, Marcus Antonius, the half partner of the empire of Rome, and Appius Claudius, the decemvir and lawgiver; whereof the former was indeed a **voluptuous** man, and **inordinate**; but the latter was an **austere** and wise man: and therefore it seems (though rarely) that love can find entrance, not only into an open heart, but also into a heart well **fortified**, if watch be not well kept.

It is a poor saying of Epicurus, Satis magnum alter alteri theatrum sumus; as if man, made for the **contemplation** of heaven, and all noble objects, should

舞台上的爱情比生活中的爱情要可观多了。因为在舞台上，爱情可以为喜剧提供素材，有时又可以给悲剧提供；而在现实生活中，爱情却常常带来严重的损害。它有时像个蛊惑人心的魔女，有时又像是一心复仇的神女。

你可以发现，一切真正伟大的人物（无论是古人还是今人，他们会被世人铭记），没有一个因爱情而发狂。因为强大的精神和伟大的事业会排除这种不堪一击的感情。不过罗马的安东尼和克劳底亚是例外，一个是执行官，另一个是法律制定者。前者本性就好色荒淫，而后者却严谨睿智。因此爱情似乎（尽管不太充分）不仅会占领胸怀开阔之人的心，有时也能闯入戒备森严的心灵——如果防守略有松懈的话。

埃辟克拉斯曾说过一句笨话："人生不过是一座大戏台。"似乎本应努力追求高尚事业的人类，却跪在自己小小的偶像面前做奴隶。尽管爱情的奴隶不同于那只顾吃喝的禽

do nothing but kneel before a little idol, and make himself a subject, though not of the mouth (as beasts are), yet of the eye; which was given him for higher purposes.

It is a strange thing, to note the excess of this passion, and how it braves the nature, and value of things, by this; that the speaking in a perpetual hyperbole, is comely in nothing but in love. Neither is it merely in the phrase; for whereas it hath been well said, that the arch-flatterer, with whom all the petty flatterers have intelligence, is a man's self; certainly the lover is more. For there was never proud man thought so absurdly well of himself, as the lover doth of the person loved; and therefore it was well said, That it is impossible to love, and to be wise. Neither doth this weakness appear to others only, and not to the party loved; but to the loved most of all, except the love be reciprocal. For it is a true rule, that love is ever rewarded, either with the reciprocal, or with an inward and secret contempt.

兽，但也是受制于入眼的色相皮囊而眼睛本来是有更高贵的用途的。

奇怪的是，过度地追求爱情会降低人本身的价值。言辞中那些被夸大了的美好，永远只存在于爱情中。这不仅仅是一句话，鉴于古人有一句名言："最大的奉承，人总是留给自己的"，但显然，对情人的奉承要算例外。因为甚至最骄傲的人，也甘愿在情人面前放低姿态。所以古人说得好："爱情与睿智二者不可兼得。"这种弱点不仅在外人看来是明显的，在被爱的一方看来也会很明显，而且是看得最明显的——除非爱是相互的。爱情是有回报或是代价的，如果得不到对方爱的回馈，就会得到一种深藏于心的轻蔑，这是一条永真的定律。

单词解析 Word Analysis

behold [bɪˈhəʊld] v 看到，注视

例 Her face was a joy to behold.
她的容貌十分悦目。

On Love 论爱情

siren ['saɪrən] *n.* 妖冶而危险的女人；塞壬（古希腊传说中半人半鸟的女海妖，诱导水手触礁或驶入危险水域）

例 The government must resist the siren voices calling for tax cuts.
政府万万不可听信那些鼓吹减税的动听言辞。

fury ['fjʊəri] *n.* 狂怒；[罗神]复仇三女神之一

例 Her eyes blazed with fury.
她的双眼迸发出暴怒之火。

voluptuous [vəˈlʌptʃuəs] *adj.* 骄奢淫逸的

例 The nobility led voluptuous lives.
贵族阶层过着骄奢淫逸的生活。

inordinate [ɪnˈɔːdɪnət] *adj.* 过度的；无节制的

例 They spend an inordinate amount of time talking.
他们花在说上的时间太多了。

austere [ɒˈstɪə(r)] *adj.* 严肃的；严厉的

例 My father was a distant, austere man.
我父亲是个难以接近的严肃的人。

fortify ['fɔːtɪfaɪ] *v.* 加强，增强

例 He fortified himself against the cold with a hot drink.
他喝了一杯热饮御寒。

contemplation [ˌkɒntəmˈpleɪʃn] *n.* 注视；凝视；沉思

例 He sat there deep in contemplation.
他坐在那里沉思着。

语法知识点 Grammar Points

① For as to the stage, love is ever matter of comedies, and now and then of tragedies; but in life it doth much mischief; sometimes like a siren, sometimes like a fury.

此句中涉及了典故（Allusion）的修辞手法，运用神话、传说、名篇里面的典故来丰富文章的文采，可以更简练地表达句意，其形式可以是单词、短语，甚至是句子。句中运用蛊惑人心的魔女和一心复仇的神女的典故来表达爱情具有魅惑复杂等特点。

例 I have nourished a viper in my bosom.
  我养了一个白眼狼。（引用了《伊索寓言》中《农夫与蛇》的典故）

② **It is a poor saying of Epicurus, Satis magnum alter alteri theatrum sumus**

"poor"贫穷的，贫乏的，可怜的，在这里可以把a poor saying理解成戏言。"Satis magnum alter alteri theatrum sumus"意思为：人生不过是一座大戏台。

③ **Neither is it merely in the phrase; for whereas it hath been well said, that the arch-flatterer, with whom all the petty flatterers have intelligence, is a man's self; certainly the lover is more.**

"Neither"置于句首，句子要完全倒装，正常语序应为："it is neither merely in the phrase"，that引导宾语从句，作said的宾语。
arch-flatterer 主要的奉承者
petty-flatters 吝啬的奉承者

经典名句 Famous Classics

1. What then in love can women do? If we grow fond they shun us. And when we fly them, they pursue; but leave us when they've won us.
   恋爱中的女人会怎么做呢？如果我们有了爱意，她们遁而避之；我们避而远之，她们又紧追不舍。当我们深陷其中时，她们却又离我们而去。

2. Love sought is good, but given unsought is better.
   追求爱情固然美好，但不经意降临的爱更美好。

3. Don't try so hard, the best things come when you least expect them to.
   不用强求，最好的总在最不经意时出现。

4. If you leave me, please don't comfort me because each sewing has to meet stinging pain.
   如果你离开我就别再来安慰我，要知道每次缝补都意味着遭遇刺穿的痛。

5. Good love makes you see the whole world from one person while bad love makes you abandon the whole world for one person.
   好的爱情让你通过一个人看到整个世界，而坏的爱情令你为了一个人舍弃整个世界。

6. Maybe God wants us to meet a few wrong people before meeting the right one, so that when we finally meet the person, we will know how to be grateful.
   在遇到正确的人之前，上帝也许会让我们先遇到几个不合适的人。这样，当我们最后遇到那个对的人之时，才会懂得感激。

7. Perfect love is rare indeed—for to be a lover will require that you continually have the subtlety of the very wise, the flexibility of the child, the sensitivity of the artists, the understanding of the philosopher, the acceptance of the saint, the tolerance of the scholar and the fortitude of the certain.
   完美的爱情并不常见，因为要做一个爱人你就必须具备智者的敏锐、少儿的灵活、艺术家的敏感、哲人的体谅、圣人的大度、学者的宽容和坚定之人的刚毅。

读书笔记

25 Pamela
帕米拉

My dear father and mother,

We arrived here last night, highly pleased with our journey, and the occasion of it. May God bless you both with long life and health, to enjoy your sweet farm, and pretty dwelling, which is just what I wished it to be. And don't make your grateful hearts too uneasy in the possession of it, by your modest **diffidence** of your own unworthiness: for, at the same time, that it is what will do honour to the best of men, it is not so very extraordinary, considering his condition, as to cause any one to **censure** it as the effect of a too partial and **injudicious** kindness for the parents of one whom he delighteth to honour.

My dear master (why should I not still call him so, bound to **reverence** him as I am, in every light he can shine in to the most obliged and sensible heart?) still proposes to fit up the large **parlour** and three apartments in the commodious dwelling he calls yours, for his entertainment and mine, when I pay my duty to you both, for a few happy days; and he has actually given orders to that effect; and that the three

我亲爱的爸爸和妈妈，

我们昨晚抵达这里，对我们的旅程本身及其时间感到非常满意。愿上帝保佑您二老长命百岁、身体健康，尽情享受你们美好的农场和美丽的居所，正如我所希望的那样。你们不要因为感激或过于谦虚不自信而不愿接受它；同时，这是授予最好的人的荣誉。鉴于他的情况，这并不算是太好，这样就没有人会指责他对喜欢之人的父母过于偏心，说他不明智。

我亲爱的主人（为什么我不应该这样称呼他来表达对他的尊敬？他在散发着光芒，能照亮每一个敏感的心里。）仍然建议装修那个带着一个客厅和三间公寓的宽敞的住宅，他称呼那个住宅为你们的住宅，这是我和他的一份心意，我也尽尽孝心，让你们过几天幸福的日子。他已经为此发出了命令，而且这三间公寓装修得太好了，相比于他自己更适合你们居住。因为他说，房间要简洁雅致，家具也需如此，这是他退休到此的不同之处。这样

apartments be so fitted up, as to be rather suitable to your condition, than his own; for, he says, the plain simple elegance, which he will have observed in the Rooms as well as the furniture, will be a variety in his retirement to this place, that will make him return to his own with the greater pleasure; and at the same time, when we are not there, will be of use for the reception of any of your friends; and so he shall not, as he kindly says, rob the good couple of any of their accommodations.

他会找回自己，更加快乐。同时，当我们不在那里时，可以用它来接待你们的朋友；所以他善意地说，他绝不会抢占一对佳偶的任何住所。

单词解析 Word Analysis

diffidence ['dɪfɪdəns] *n.* 缺乏自信

例 He entered the room with a certain diffidence.
他怯生生地走进房间。

censure ['senʃə(r)] *v.* 指责；谴责；责备；批评

例 He was censured for leaking information to the press.
他因泄漏消息给新闻界而受到谴责。

injudicious [ˌɪndʒuˈdɪʃəs] *adj.* 判断不当的，不聪明的

例 He blamed injudicious comments by bankers for last week's devaluation.
他将上周的货币贬值归咎于银行家所做的不当评论。

reverence ['revərəns] *v.* 尊敬；崇敬；敬畏

例 We reverence tradition but will not be fettered by it.
我们尊重传统，但不被传统所束缚。

我的名著美文：人不是生来就要被打败的

parlour ['pɑːlə(r)] *n.* 客厅，会客室

例 He went very aggressively into the parlour.
他挑衅地闯进客厅。

语法知识点 *Grammar Points*

① **May God bless you both with long life and health, to enjoy your sweet farm, and pretty dwelling, which is just what I wished it to be.**

"May God bless..."是表示祝福的句型，为倒装语序。

例 May God bless our country and all who defend her.
上帝保佑我们的国家，保佑我们的战士们。

② **...it is not so very extraordinary, considering his condition, as to cause any one to censure it as the effect of a too partial and injudicious kindness for the parents of one whom he delighteth to honour.**

"considering his condition"考虑到他的情况，鉴于他的情况；在本句中作插入语。

"so +adj. + as to"如此……以至于……

例 The canyon was so beautiful as to describe.
峡谷美丽无比，非言语所能形容。

③ **...and that the three apartments be so fitted up, as to be rather suitable to your condition, than his own**

"so +adj. + as to"如此……以至于……

"be fitted up"装修

例 It turned out to be very handsomely fitted up.
它装修完非常漂亮。

"be suitable to"适合……

例 This wine is not suitable to my taste.
这酒不合我的胃口。

经典名句 Famous Classics

1. The comforter's head never aches.
   会安慰的人从不头痛。

2. The couch is the idle man's prison.
   沙发是懒人的牢笼。

3. Do not ape your betters.
   不要刻意模仿比你强的人。

4. Do not despise your enemy.
   不可轻敌。

5. People do not lack strength; they lack will.
   人们不缺力量，缺的是决心。

6. The exception proves the rule.
   规矩也有例外。

7. No news is good news.
   没有消息就是好消息。

8. Do one's level best.
   尽力而为。

9. None are so deaf as those who will not hear.
   聋子不算聋，有耳无听才是聋。

读书笔记

26 Pride and Prejudice
傲慢与偏见

It is a truth universally acknowledged, that a single man **in possession of** a good fortune must be in want of a wife.

However little known the feelings or views of such a man may be on his first entering a **neighbourhood**, this truth is so well fixed in the minds of the surrounding families, that he is considered as the **rightful** property of some one or other of their daughters.

"My dear Mr. Bennet," said his lady to him one day, "have you heard that Netherfield Park is let at last?"

Mr. Bennet replied that he had not.

"But it is," returned she; "for Mrs. Long has just been here, and she told me all about it."

Mr. Bennet made no answer.

"Do not you want to know who has taken it?" cried his wife impatiently.

"You want to tell me, and I have no objection to hearing it."

This was invitation enough.

"Why, my dear, you must know, Mrs. Long says that Netherfield is taken by a young man of large fortune from the north of England; that he came down on Monday in a chaise and

凡是有钱的单身汉，总要娶位太太，这是一条举世公认的真理。

这样的单身汉，每逢新搬到一个地方，尽管四邻八舍基本上不了解他的性情如何，见解如何，但由于这样的一条真理早已在人们心中根深蒂固，人们总是把他视为自己某一个女儿理所应得的一笔财产。

一天，班纳特太太对她的丈夫说："我的好老爷，尼日斐花园终于租出去了，你听说了吗？"

班纳特先生回答说他不知道。

"的确租出去了，"她说，"朗格太太刚刚上这儿来，把这件事的来龙去脉一五一十地和我说了。"

班纳特先生没有理睬她。

"你难道不想知道是谁租去的吗？"班纳特太太不耐烦地嚷叫起来。

"你想说给我听，那我听听也无妨。"

这句话足够鼓励她讲下去了。

four to see the place, and was so much **delighted** with it that he agreed with Mr. Morris immediately; that he is to take possession before Michaelmas, and some of his servants are to be in the house by the end of next week."

"What is his name?"

"Bingley."

"Is he married or single?"

"Oh! single, my dear, to be sure! A single man of large fortune; four or five thousand a year. What a fine thing for our girls!"

"How so? How can it affect them?"

"My dear Mr. Bennet," replied his wife, "how can you be so **tiresome**! You must know that I am thinking of his marrying one of them."

"Is that his design in settling here?"

"Design! nonsense, how can you talk so! But it is very likely that he may fall in love with one of them, and therefore you must visit him as soon as he comes."

"哦！亲爱的，你得知道，朗格太太说，租尼日斐花园的是个来自英格兰北部的阔少爷；他星期一那天，乘着一辆由四匹马拉的马车来看房子，看得非常中意，当场就和莫理斯先生谈妥了，他要在'米迦勒节'以前搬进来，打算先叫几个佣人在下个周末之前住进去。"

"他叫什么名字？"

"宾利。"

"他是已婚了还是单身状态？"

"噢！单身状态，亲爱的，他确确实实是个单身汉！一个非常有钱的单身汉，每年有四五千英镑的收入。对女儿们来说真是件大好事儿！"

"这怎么说？关女儿们什么事？"

"我的好老爷，"太太回答道，"你怎么这么不开窍！告诉你吧，我正在盘算，他和我们的一个女儿结为夫妻！"

"他住到这儿来，就是为了这个打算吗？"

"打算！胡扯，这是哪儿的话！不过，他极有可能爱上我们的某一个女儿。这样的话，他一搬来，你就得去拜访拜访他。"

115

我的名著美文：人不是生来就要被打败的

单词解析 Word Analysis

possession [pəˈzeʃn] *n.* 拥有；具有
in possession of 拥有，持有；占据

例 Their opponents were in possession of the ball for most of the match.
他们的对手在比赛的大部分时间里都控制着球。

rightful [ˈraitfl] *adj.* 合法的；正当的

例 The painting has been returned to its rightful owner.
那幅画已经归还给它的合法持有人了。

delighted [diˈlaitid] *adj.* 高兴的；愉悦的；快乐的

例 I was delighted with my presents I had received.
我对自己收到的礼物很满意。

tiresome [ˈtaiəsəm] *adj.* 令人生厌的；无聊的

例 It would be too tiresome to wait in a long queue.
排长队等候实在是令人厌烦。

语法知识点 Grammar Points

① **It is a truth universally acknowledged, that a single man in possession of a good fortune must be in want of a wife.**

此句句型为主语从句，it作形式主语，真正的主语为"a single man in possession of a good fortune must be in want of a wife"。"in want of"需要，缺少。

例 A rich person is seldom in want of a friend.
富在深山有远亲。

② **However little known the feelings or views of such a man may be on his first entering a neighbourhood, this truth is so well fixed in the minds of the surrounding families, that he is considered as the rightful property of some one or other of their daughters.**

此句话是由"however"引导的让步状语从句,表示"无论多么"。
"that"引导的是同位语从句,由that引出的所有是"this truth"的同位语。
"be fixed in"固定在

例 Leonard was now fixed in his mind.
兰纳德现在让他无法忘怀了。

> ③ Mrs. Long says that Netherfield is taken by a young man of large fortune from the north of England; that he came down on Monday in a chaise and four to see the place, and was so much delighted with it that he agreed with Mr. Morris immediately; that he is to take possession before Michaelmas, and some of his servants are to be in the house by the end of next week.

此长句句型为"sb. says that...; that...; that..."本句话中的三个"that"表并列,均为表语从句。
"a young man of large fortune"是文学表达方式,表示"一位有钱的年轻人"。

经典名句 Famous Classics

1. Love the heart that hurts you, but never hurt the heart that loves you.
   纵然你爱的人伤害了你,千万不要伤害爱你的人。

2. If you find someone else in love with you and you don't love him or her, feel honored that love came and called at your door, but gently refuse the gift you cannot return.
   如果有人爱上了你,而你却不能报之以爱,你应为爱情的来临感到荣幸,但是你要温柔地拒绝这份无法回报的礼物。

3. First love is only a little foolishness and a lot of curiosity.
   初恋只是一点点愚蠢加上许许多多的好奇。

4. We only love truly once. It is the first time and succeeding passions are less uncontrolled.
   真爱只有一次,那就是初恋。在那之后,感情就不那么无羁无绊了。

5. The magic of first love is our ignorance that it can never end.
   初恋的魔力在于我们不知道它一直不会结束。

6. First love is unforgettable all one's life.
   初恋永生难忘。

7. Love's like the measles—all the worse when it comes late in life.
   爱情犹如麻疹——来得晚,糟得很。

8. Love, with very young people, is a heartless business. We drink at that age from thirst, or to get drunk; it is only later in life that we occupy ourselves with the individuality of our wine.
   对于年轻人而言,恋爱是一件无情的事情。年轻时,我们渴了就饮(酒),甚至沉醉其中;只有年长后才一心嗜好自家的酒。

读书笔记

27 Sense and Sensibility
理智与情感

The family of Dashwood had long been settled in Sussex. Their **estate** was large, and their residence was at Norland Park, in the centre of their property, where, for many generations, they had lived in so respectable a manner as to engage the general good opinion of their surrounding acquaintance. The late owner of this estate was a single man, who lived to a very advanced age, and who for many years of his life, had a constant companion and housekeeper in his sister. But her death, which happened ten years before his own, produced a great **alteration** in his home; for to supply her loss, he invited and received into his house the family of his nephew Mr. Henry Dashwood, the legal **inheritor** of the Norland estate, and the person to whom he intended to **bequeath** it. In the society of his nephew and niece, and their children, the old Gentleman's days were comfortably spent. His **attachment** to them all increased. The constant attention of Mr. and Mrs. Henry Dashwood to his wishes, which proceeded not merely from interest, but from goodness of heart, gave him every degree of solid comfort which his age could receive; and

达什伍德一家在苏塞克斯定居可有些时日了。家里置下一个偌大的房产，府第就设在田庄中心的诺兰庄园。祖祖辈辈以来，一家人一直在那儿过着体面的日子，赢得了乡邻的赞誉。已故庄园主是个单身汉，活了一大把年纪。他有生之年的大部分时间，妹妹都陪着他，替他打理家务。不想妹妹早他十年去世，致使府上发生巨变。为了填补妹妹的空缺，他将侄儿亨利·达什伍德一家接到府上。老达什伍德打算把家业传给亨利·达什伍德先生，这个诺兰田庄的法定继承人。这位老绅士有侄儿、侄媳及其子女相伴，日子过得舒适安逸。他越来越喜爱他们。亨利·达什伍德夫妇不仅是出于利益考虑，也是由于心地善良，对他总是百般照应，使他得以颐养天年。而那群天真烂漫的孩子们也给他的生活增添了乐趣。

亨利·达什伍德先生同前妻生下一个儿子，同现任妻子生了三个女儿。儿子是个踏实体面的青年。他母亲留下了一

the cheerfulness of the children added a **relish** to his existence.

By a former marriage, Mr. Henry Dashwood had one son: by his present lady, three daughters. The son, a steady respectable young man, was **amply** provided for by the fortune of his mother, which had been large, and half of which **devolved** on him on his coming of age. By his own marriage, likewise, which happened soon afterwards, he added to his wealth. To him therefore the succession to the Norland estate was not so really important as to his sisters; for their fortune, independent of what might arise to them from their father's inheriting that property, could be but small. Their mother had nothing, and their father only seven thousand pounds in his own disposal; for the remaining moiety of his first wife's fortune was also secured to her child, and he had only a life-interest in it.

大笔遗产，他成年后有一半转到了他的名下。此后不久，他成了亲，同样地，他又增添了一笔财产。所以，对他说来，父亲继承诺兰田庄与否，远不像对他几个妹妹那样紧要。这几个妹妹假若不依赖父亲继承这笔家业进而可以给她们带来的家业，她们的财产将少得可怜。她们的母亲一无所有，父亲仅仅掌管着七千镑，而对前妻另一半遗产的所有权只在生前有效，他一去世，这一半财产也归儿子承袭。

单词解析 Word Analysis

estate [iˈsteit] *n.* 房地产；财产

例 We went straight to the estate agent and wrote a cheque.
我们径直走向房产经纪人那儿开了一张支票。

alteration [ˌɔːltəˈreiʃn] *n.* 变化；改变

例 The shirt needs alteration.
这件衬衫需要改动。

inheritor [inˈherɪtə(r)] *n.* 继承人；后继者

例 Later, the little monk became the inheritor of the master.
后来，这位小和尚继承了大师的衣钵。

bequeath [bɪˈkwiːð] *v.* （在遗嘱中）把……赠送给
bequeath sth. to sb./bequeath sb. sth. （在遗嘱中）把……赠送给

例 He bequeathed his entire estate to his daughter.
他把全部财产都遗赠给女儿了。

attachment [əˈtætʃmənt] *n.* 爱慕；依恋

例 A child has strong attachments to their parents.
孩子对父母有强烈的依赖感。

relish [ˈrelɪʃ] *n.* 享受；乐趣

例 She savoured the moment with obvious relish.
显然，她津津有味地回味那一刻。

amply [ˈæmpli] *adv.* 充足地；详细地

例 They have been amply rewarded with huge salaries.
他们得到了丰厚的回报——高薪。

devolve [dɪˈvɒlv] *v.* 移交；转移；交给
devolve on/upon sb./sth. （财产、金钱等遗产）转给，传给，移交；（职责、责任等）交由……接替，委托……承担

例 The house will devolve to his daughter.
这个房子将由他女儿继承。

语法知识点 Grammar Points

① Their estate was large, and their residence was at Norland Park, in the centre of their property, where, for many generations, they had lived in so respectable a manner as to engage the general good opinion of their surrounding acquaintance.

此句中有两个插入语：in the centre of their property 和 for many generations，"where" 引导地点状语从句，表示"在……"。

"so+ adj. +as to" 如此……以至于……

例 Yesterday morning I got up so late as to be late for school.
昨天早晨我起得那么晚，上学都迟到了。

② **The late owner of this estate was a single man, who lived to a very advanced age, and who for many years of his life, had a constant companion and housekeeper in his sister.**

"live to" 活到……

例 Many people have a wish to live to old age.
许多人想长寿。

"a constant companion and housekeeper in his sister" 中有一个限定词：不定冠词a，以及companion 和housekeeper，都是指代妹妹，妹妹既是陪伴者又是管家者。

例 She is a singer and dancer.
她是一个唱跳型歌手。

③ **...for to supply her loss, he invited and received into his house the family of his nephew Mr. Henry Dashwood, the legal inheritor of the Norland estate, and the person to whom he intended to bequeath it.**

"the legal inheritor of the Norland estate" 和 "and the person to whom he intended to bequeath it" 均为 "Mr. Henry Dashwood" 的同位语，对其进行解释说明。

"and the person to whom he intended to bequeath it" 中有whom引导的宾语从句，实际上的顺序应为 "and he intended to bequeath it to the person" 。

④ **...for their fortune, independent of what might arise to them from their father's inheriting that property, could be but small.**

"independent of what might arise to them from their father's inheriting that property" 作插入语，应为for their fortune could be but small。
be independent of 不依赖于……，独立于……

例 Judges must be independent of political pressure.
法官们一定不能受政治压力影响。

经典名句 Famous Classics

1. Do not keep all your eggs in one basket.
   不要把鸡蛋全都放在一个篮子里。

2. Do not through fear of poverty surrender liberty.
   不要因为害怕贫穷而放弃自由。

3. The course of true love never did run smooth.
   爱情之路无坦途。（好事多磨。）

4. The cow knows not what her tail is worth until she has lost it.
   有时不爱惜，失后徒叹息。

5. The eye that sees all things else sees not itself.
   智者千虑，必有一失。

6. The eye will be where the love is.
   目光总是跟着所爱的人走。

7. No man learns but by pain or shame.
   不经痛苦羞辱，难以取得教训。

8. No medicine can cure a man of discontent.
   有药难治不满之人。

读书笔记

28 Sister Carrie
嘉莉妹妹

When a girl leaves her home at eighteen, she does one of two things. Either she falls into saving hands and becomes better, or she rapidly assumes the **cosmopolitan** standard of virtue and becomes worse. Of an intermediate balance, under the circumstances, there is no possibility. The city has its cunning wiles, no less than the infinitely smaller and more human tempter. There are large forces which **allure** with all the soulfulness of expression possible in the most cultured human. The **gleam** of a thousand lights is often as effective as the persuasive light in a wooing and fascinating eye. Half the undoing of the unsophisticated and natural mind is accomplished by forces wholly superhuman. A blare of sound, a roar of life, a vast array of human hives, appeal to the astonished senses in **equivocal** terms. Without a counsellor at hand to whisper cautious interpretations, what falsehoods may not these things breathe into the unguarded ear! Unrecognised for what they are, their beauty, like music, too often relaxes, then weakens, then **perverts** the simpler human

当一个女孩十八岁离家踏上人生征程时，结局不外乎两种。要么她遇到好人相助，变得更好；要么随波逐流，从而变得更糟。二者必须择其一，在这种情况下，想要不好不坏、保持中间状态是不可能的。这个城市有种种诱人的花招，它绝不亚于那些唆使人们学坏的男男女女。城市有强大的魔力，能用最有学识的人才能表达的华丽辞藻使人迷乱。都市的灯火阑珊和含情脉脉又迷人的眼睛一样有效。有一半涉世未深的单纯心灵是被非人为的力量摧毁的。人声鼎沸、热闹的生活、鳞次栉比的高楼，这一切都令人惊愕又具有极强的吸引力，也不知道是哪种情绪多一点。如果没有人在身边轻声告诫解说，又有什么样的谎言和谬误不会灌入这些不加提防之人的耳朵里呢！头脑简单的人不能对它们有正确的认识，会为它们的美所倾倒，就如同音乐一样，它们先使人放松，接着削弱意志，最后使人堕落。

perceptions.

    Caroline, or Sister Carrie, as she had been half affectionately termed by the family, was possessed of a mind **rudimentary** in its power of observation and analysis. Self-interest with her was high, but not strong. It was, nevertheless, her guiding characteristic. Warm with the fancies of youth, pretty with the **insipid** prettiness of the formative period, possessed of a figure promising eventual shapeliness and an eye alight with certain native intelligence, she was a fair example of the middle American class--two generations removed from the emigrant. Books were beyond her interest--knowledge a sealed book. In the intuitive graces she was still crude. She could scarcely toss her head gracefully. Her hands were almost ineffectual. The feet, though small, were set flatly. And yet she was interested in her charms, quick to understand the keener pleasures of life, ambitious to gain in material things. A half-equipped little knight she was, venturing to **reconnoitre** the mysterious city and dreaming wild dreams of some vague, far-off supremacy, which should make it prey and subject-the proper penitent, groveling at a woman's slipper.

    嘉洛琳，家人带着几分疼爱地称呼她为嘉莉妹妹，已经拥有基本的观察能力和分析能力。她的利己心，但并不是很强。不过，这是她的主要特点。她富于年轻人的热烈幻想；有着处于发育时期的清新之美；从现在的身段就可以看出她将来发育完全时的曼妙身姿；眼中透露着几分天生的聪慧。她是一个典型的美国中产阶级少女——她们家已经是移民的第三代了。她对书籍不感兴趣——书本知识是一本密封的书。她的举手投足、一言一行都依靠自己的本能进行，因此略显粗野。她甩头的姿势不够优雅；她的手几乎没有什么用处；尽管她的脚小巧，但也只会平放。然而，她对自己的魅力很感兴趣，可以很快感知生活中更加强烈的乐趣，并且渴望物质的享受。她是一个没有完全装备的小骑士，正在试图侦察这个神秘的城市，梦想着一些模糊又遥远的至高地位，让大城市成为服从的猎物，跪在她的脚下俯首称臣。

单词解析 Word Analysis

cosmopolitan [ˌkɒzməˈpɒlɪtən] *adj.* 世界性的，全世界的

例 The family are rich, and extremely sophisticated and cosmopolitan.
这家人很富有，老于世故，而且见多识广。

allure [əˈlʊə(r)] *v.* 引诱，诱惑

例 He generally shunned the traps there were laid to allure him into discussion.
他一般会避开诱导他讨论的那些陷阱。

gleam [gliːm] *n.* 闪光，闪亮

例 There was a gleam of hope for a peaceful settlement.
还有一线和平解决的希望。

equivocal [ɪˈkwɪvəkl] *adj.* 模棱两可的；意义不明的

例 She gave an equivocal answer, typical of a politician.
她的回答模棱两可，是典型的政客做法。

pervert [pəˈvɜːt] *v.* 使堕落；误用，滥用

例 He was charged with conspiring to pervert the course of justice.
他被控谋划妨碍司法公正。

rudimentary [ˌruːdɪˈmentri] *adj.* 基本的，初步的

例 He has only a rudimentary knowledge of French.
他对法语只是略知皮毛。

insipid [ɪnˈsɪpɪd] *adj.* 枯燥的，无生气的

例 After an hour of insipid conversation, I left.
经过一个小时乏味的谈话之后，我离开了。

reconnoitre [ˌrekəˈnɔɪtə(r)] *v.* 侦察，勘探

例 He was sent to reconnoitre the enemy position.
他被派去侦察敌军位置。

语法知识点 *Grammar Points*

① **When a girl leaves her home at eighteen, she does one of two things. Either she falls into saving hands and becomes better, or she rapidly assumes the cosmopolitan standard of virtue and becomes worse.**

"either...or"表示二者则一，"不是……就是，……或者……"。

例 He seems either to fear women or to sentimentalize them.
他似乎要么怕女人要么就对她们怀有浪漫想法。

"fall into" 分成

例 The chapter falls into three sections.
这一章共分三节。

② **Without a counsellor at hand to whisper cautious interpretations, what falsehoods may not these things breathe into the unguarded ear!**

此句话中涉及了移就修辞法（Transferred Epithet）。"the unguarded ear"中的unguarded修饰的不是ear，而是人，可译为"不加防范之人"

例 After an unthinking moment, she put her pen in her mouth.
一不留神，她把笔放进了嘴里。（unthinking修饰的不是moment，而是she）

例 The host handed me a hospitable glass of wine.
东道主非常好客，递了一杯红酒给我。（hospitable修饰的不是glass of wine，而是the host）

③ **Unrecognised for what they are, their beauty, like music, too often relaxes, then weakens, then perverts the simpler human perceptions.**

本句中涉及明喻的修辞方法（Simile），可译为"像……，如同……"。

例 Youth slips away like flowing water.
年华似水。

例 act money like dirt 挥金如土

经典名句 Famous Classics

1. The evil [evils] we bring on ourselves is [are] hardest to bear.
   自找之罪最难受。

2. The excellence of a wife consists not in her beauty, but in her virtue.
   妻贤在德不在貌。

3. The eye is bigger than the belly.
   眼大肚皮小。

4. Do well and have well.
   善有善报。

5. The fairest silk is soonest soiled.
   最洁白的丝绸脏得最快。

6. The best ability is dependability.
   最佳能力是"可靠"。

7. One year a nurse, and seven years the worse.
   一年当保姆，七年成懒妇。

8. Only that which is honestly got is gain.
   正当的收入才是真正的收入。

读书笔记

29 Tender is the Night
夜色温柔

He confirmed this decision walking around the rays of late afternoon in his work-room. With the new plan he could be through by spring. It seemed to him that when a man with his energy was pursued for a year by increasing doubts, it indicated some fault in the plan.

……

He saw Nicole in the garden. Presently he must encounter her and the prospect gave him a **leaden** feeling. Before her he must keep up a perfect front, now and tomorrow, next week and next year. All night in Paris he had held her in his arms while she slept light under the **luminol**; in the early morning he broke in upon her confusion before it could form, with words of tenderness and protection, and she slept again with his face against the warm scent of her hair. Before she woke he had arranged everything at the phone in the next room. Rosemary was to move to another hotel. She was to be "Daddy's Girl"and even to give up saying goodbye to them. The **proprietor** of the hotel, Mr. McBeth, was to be the three Chinese monkeys. Packing amid the piled boxes and tissue

午后的阳光照进工作室，他一边踱步一边斟酌这项决定。有了这个新计划，他可能在春天前就完成。在他看来，如果在一年中，一个精力充沛的人被越来越多的疑虑困扰着，那就表明计划本身有缺陷。

……

他在花园里看到了尼科尔。不一会就要和她见面，想到这儿他心里沉甸甸的。在她面前，他必须保持一个完美的形象，无论是现在、明天、下周或是明年，都要如此。在巴黎，他整夜把她拥在臂弯里，而服用了镇静剂的她也只是在浅眠；一大清早，他便温声细语不让她困惑不安，就这样她再次入睡，而他的脸抵着她温暖的发香。在她醒来前，他已经在隔壁通过电话把一切都安排好了。萝丝玛丽要搬到另一家旅馆。她将成为"老爸的女儿"，甚至没有向他们道别。酒店的所有者麦克贝斯先生将忙得焦头烂额。在堆积成山的箱子和纸巾这些采购物中，狄克和尼科尔收拾行李，中午乘

paper of many purchases, Dick and Nicole left for the Riviera at noon.

Then there was a reaction. As they settled down in the wagon-lit Dick saw that Nicole was waiting for it, and it came quickly and desperately, before the train was out of the ceinture—his only instinct was to step off while the train was still going slow, rush back and see where Rosemary was, what she was doing. He opened a book and bent his **pince-nez** upon it, aware that Nicole was watching him from her pillow across the **compartment**. Unable to read, he pretended to be tired and shut his eyes but she was still watching him, and though still she was half asleep from the **hangover** of the drug, she was relieved and almost happy that he was hers again.

船去里维埃拉。

这时，有了一种反应。当他们在火车上安顿下来时，迪克明白尼科尔正在期待着。在火车熄灭之前，这反应来得迅速又猛烈——他唯一的本能就是在火车还在缓慢行进时跳下去，回去看看萝丝玛丽在哪里，在做些什么。他打开一本书，将他的夹鼻眼镜压在上面，意识到尼科尔正在靠着车厢对面的枕头看着他。他无法看书，便假装累了，闭上了眼睛，但她仍然在注视着他。尽管她由于服了药，整个人晕乎乎的，但她感觉轻松，甚至是开心，因为他又是她的了。

单词解析 Word Analysis

leaden ['ledn] *adj.* 沉重的；沉闷的；阴沉的

例 A leaden weight lay on her heart as she waved him goodbye.
她向他挥手道别时，心情十分沉重。

luminol ['luːminəl] *n.* 发光氨

例 A chemical reaction occurs when luminol comes into contact with hemoglobin, an oxygen-carrying protein in blood.
当发光氨与血色素血液中一种含氧的蛋白质接触后就会发生化学作用。

proprietor [prə'praiəti] *n.* 所有人；业主

例 He is the sole proprietor of this company now.
这家公司现在归他一人所有。

Tender is the Night 夜色温柔 29

pince-nez ['pænsnei] *n.* 夹鼻眼镜

例 His secretary was a tall lady in pince-nez.
他的秘书是位戴着夹鼻眼镜的高个子女士。

compartment [kəm'pa:tmənt] *n.* 隔间；隔层

例 The desk has a secret compartment.
这张桌子有一个暗格。

hangover ['hæŋəuvə(r)] *n.* 宿醉；遗留下来的感觉、风俗或思想

例 He is still sleeping off the hangover of yesterday.
他还在睡觉以便消除昨晚的宿醉。

语法知识点 Grammar Points

① **He confirmed this decision walking around the rays of late afternoon in his work-room.**

"confirm sth./that +从句"证实，证明，确认。

例 Earlier reports were unable to confirm that there were any survivors.
先前的报道无法证实是否有幸存者。

"walk around"四处闲逛，在本句中为非谓语动词，表示主动。

例 He was walking around with a sad face.
他四处走着，神色哀伤。

② **It seemed to him that when a man with his energy was pursued for a year by increasing doubts, it indicated some fault in the plan.**

"it seems (to sb.)+that"（在某人看来）似乎……，好像……

例 It seems to me that he has known nothing of life.
在我看来，他还不懂人情世故。

"when"引导时间状语从句，表示"当……"。

③ **Presently he must encounter her and the prospect gave him a leaden feeling.**

"presently"不久，马上，目前，放句首引导整个句子。

131

例 Presently, a young woman in white came in.
　　不久，一位穿白衣的女子进来了。

"give sb. a feeling of +adj." 使某人有……的感觉

例 Rainy days give me a feeling of melancholy.
　　雨天给我一种忧郁的感觉。

④ **The proprietor of the hotel, Mr. McBeth, was to be the three Chinese monkeys.**

"Mr. McBeth" 是 "the proprietor of the hotel" 的同位语。
在国外的文化中，"Chinese monkeys" 指代的是有反叛精神、大闹天宫的美猴王孙悟空，the three Chinese monkeys可译为：乱糟糟的，焦头烂额。

经典名句 Famous Classics

1. The eye is blind if the mind is absent.
   心不专则眼不明。

2. The eye is the window of the heart.
   眼睛是心灵的窗户。

3. The fairest rose is at last withered.
   最美的玫瑰也会凋谢。

4. One thing well done is twice done.
   事半功倍。

5. Pity is akin to love.
   怜悯近乎爱情。

6. The brave man hazards his life, but not his conscience.
   勇敢的人可以冒险，但不可以违背良知。

7. Pride is the mask of one's faults.
   骄傲是掩饰错误的面具。

8. Procrastination is the thief of time.
   拖延就是浪费时间。

9. A busy mother makes a lazy daughter.
勤劳的母亲女儿懒。

读书笔记

30 Tess of the D'Urbervilles
德伯家的苔丝

He heard something behind him, the brush of feet. Turning, he saw over the **prostrate** columns another figure; then before he was aware, another was at hand on the right, under a trilithon, and another on the left. The dawn shone full on the front of the man westward, and Clare could **discern** from this that he was tall, and walked as if trained. They all closed in with evident purpose. Her story then was true! **Springing to** his feet, he looked around for a weapon, loose stone, means of escape, anything. By this time the nearest man was upon him.

"It is no use, sir," he said. "There are sixteen of us on the Plain, and the whole country is **reared**."

"Let her finish her sleep!" he **implored** in a whisper of the men as they gathered round.

When they saw where she lay, which they had not done till then, they showed no objection, and stood watching her, as still as the **pillars** around. He went to the stone and bent over her, holding one poor little hand; her breathing now was quick and small,

他（克莱尔）听见身后有声音，是一串脚步声。他转身就看到地上的石柱边上又来了一个人。他还没有反应过来，右边的牌坊下面又出现一个人，接着左边也出现了一个人。曙光从正面照到了西面那个男人身上，克莱尔由此判断此人身材高大，且走起路来训练有素的样子。他们又靠近了些，目的很明显。她（苔丝）之前说的是真话。克莱尔突然跳起来，四处寻找武器、石头、脱身的手段及能用上的一切。这时，离他最近的人已经来到了他面前。

"别费力气了，先生，"那个人说，"在这个平原上就有我们16个人，而且整个地区都动员起来了。"

"让她睡完觉吧！"克莱尔见那些人从四面包围了上来，便轻声乞求道。

当他们看到苔丝在那里躺着后，就没有反对克莱尔的请求，在那儿守着，就像周围的石柱一样，一动不动。克莱尔走到石板边，俯身握住她一只可怜的小手，她的呼吸短促而

like that of a lesser creature than a woman. All waited in the growing light, their faces and hands as if they were silvered, the remainder of their figures dark, the stones **glistening** green-gray, the Plain still a mass of shade. Soon the light was strong, and a ray shone upon her unconscious form, peering under her **eyelids** and waking her.

"What is it, Angel?"she said, starting up. "Have they come for me?"

"Yes, dearest,"he said. "They have come."

"It is as it should be,"she **murmured**. "Angel, I am almost glad--yes, glad! This happiness could not have lasted. It was too much. I have had enough; and now I shall not live for you to **despise** me!"

She stood up, shook herself, and went forward, neither of the men having moved.

"I am ready,"she said quietly.

轻微，像是一种比女人还弱小的生物。光线越来越亮，所有人都在等待着，他们的手和脸像镀了一层银白色；全身其他部分还是黑色的；石头泛着灰绿色的光泽；大平原仍旧是一片灰暗。很快，光线变得很强烈，一束光照在了苔丝那没有知觉的身体上，透过她的眼睑唤醒了她。

"怎么了，安吉尔？"苔丝起身，"他们来抓我了吗？"

"是的，我最亲爱的，"克莱尔说，"他们来了。"

"当然了，"她咕哝着，"安吉尔，我差不多是开心的——是的，很开心！这幸福本就不会长久，这也太幸福了。我已经很幸福了。现在，我不用等着你嫌弃我了。"

她站起身，整理了一下衣服，向前走去；那些人一个也没开始行动。

"我准备好了。"她平静地说着。

注：男主人公全名为安吉尔·克莱尔，安吉尔和克莱尔所指为同一人。

我的名著美文：人不是生来就要被打败的

单词解析 *Word Analysis*

prostrate ['prɔstreit] *adj.* 卧倒的

例 They felt prostrate in worship.
他们拜倒在地。

discern [di'sə:n] *v.* 了解，看出，辨别

例 It is possible to discern a number of different techniques in her work.
从她的作品中可以识别出许多不同的写作手法。

spring [spriŋ] *v.* 跳；蹦
spring to one's feet 跳了起来，立刻站起来

例 Everyone sprang to their feet when the principal walked in.
校长一进来，所有人都立刻站了起来。

rear [riə] *v.* （令人不快之物）出现，露头，显露

例 The threat of strikes reared its head again this summer.
今年夏天又出现了罢工的势头。

implore [im'plɔ:(r)] *v.* 恳求，哀求

例 I implore you not to leave me here.
求求你别把我留在这儿。

pillar ['pilə(r)] *n.* 石柱，台柱

例 I fell asleep against a pillar.
我靠着柱子睡着了。

glisten ['glisn] *v.* 闪耀，闪亮

例 The leaves glisten with dew.
叶子上的露水闪闪发光。

eyelid ['ailid] *n.* 眼皮，眼睑

例 Her left eyelid twitched involunratily.
她的左眼皮不由自主地抽搐起来。

murmur ['mə:mə(r)] v. 咕哝，小声说话

例 He murmured something in his sleep.
他在睡梦中嘟囔着什么。

despise [di'spaiz] v. 鄙视，看不起

例 She despised gossip in any form.
她对任何形式的流言蜚语都嗤之以鼻。

语法知识点 Grammar Points

① **They all closed in with evident purpose.**

"close in (on sb./sth.)"（尤指为了进攻）逼近，靠近

例 The lion closed in on his prey.
这只狮子逼近了猎物。

"with evident purpose"作方式状语，可译为"带有"。

② **Springing to his feet, he looked around for a weapon, loose stone, means of escape, anything.**

"look around for sth."到处寻找；搜寻。"springing to one's feet"作伴随状语，整句话的主语是he，宾语是：a weapon, loose stone, means of escape 及anything。

③ **"Let her finish her sleep!"he implored in a whisper of the men as they gathered round.**

"in a whisper"低声地

例 She said it in a whisper, so I didn't hear.
她是低声说的，所以我没有听见。

as引导时间状语从句，表示"当……时候"。

例 As she grew older she gained in confidence.
随着年龄的增长，她的信心增强了。

④ **She stood up, shook herself, and went forward, neither of the men having moved.**

整句话的主语是"she"，谓语动词为三个并列的动作：stood up, shook herself和went forward。"neither of the men having moved"是独立主格结

构，表示"没有一个人行动起来"。

经典名句 Famous Classics

1. LOVE: The irresistible desire to be irresistibly desired.
   爱情：一种无法遏制的渴望，渴望得到难以克制的爱。

2. To love and be loved is to feel the sun from both sides.
   爱与被爱就像是前后身都能感受到阳光，同样温暖。

3. To love is to place our happiness in the happiness of another.
   爱就是把我们的幸福融入另一个人的幸福之中。

4. Dog does not eat dog.
   同类不相残。

5. The best hearts are always the bravest.
   行为勇敢的人心地总是善良的。

6. The best horse needs breaking, and the aptest child needs teaching.
   好马需要训，好子需要教。

7. The best is often times the enemy of the good.
   要求过高，反难成功。

8. None but a wise man can employ leisure well.
   唯智者善于利用空闲时间。

读书笔记

31 The Adventures of Huckleberry Finn
哈克贝利·费恩历险记

I felt good and all washed clean of sin for the first time I had ever felt so in my life, and I knew I could pray now. But I didn't do it straight off, but laid the paper down and set there thinking—thinking how good it was all this happened so, and how near I come to being lost and going to hell. And went on thinking. And got to thinking over our trip down the river; and I see Jim before me all the time: in the day and in the night-time, sometimes moonlight, sometimes storms, and we floating along, talking and singing and laughing.

But somehow I couldn't seem to strike no places to harden me against him, but only the other kind. I'd see him standing my watch on top of his, instead of calling me, so I could go on sleeping; and see him how glad he was when I come back out of the fog; and when I come to him again in the **swamp**, up there where the **feud** was; and such-like times; and would always call me honey, and pet me and do everything he could think of for me, and how good he always was; and at last I struck the time I saved him by telling the men we

我觉着挺好的，觉得自己已经把所有的罪恶都清洗干净了，这是我有生以来第一次有这样的感觉。我知道，如今我可以祈祷啦。不过我没有立刻就去祈祷，而是一边把纸放好一边在回忆——想着事情发展成现在这样，这是一件多么棒的事情啊；想着我又怎样差点儿迷失方向，掉进地狱。我又想到了我们沿河而下的情景，我发现杰姆一直以来都在我的眼前：无论是在白天，还是在深夜，有时在月色下，有时在风暴中，我们沿途漂泊，一起聊天、唱歌、欢笑。

可是不管怎样我似乎找不到任何事，能叫我对他硬起心肠来。而且情况正好相反，我看到即使他才值完了班，他也不愿意前来叫我，宁愿替我值班，这样就可以让我继续睡大觉了。我看到，当我从一片浓雾中回来时他是有多高兴呀；当我从宿敌所在的沼泽地中回来去找他时，他是多么高兴；我记得这些相似的时刻；记得他总要叫我乖乖，总是宠着

had small-pox aboard, and he was so grateful, and said I was the best friend old Jim ever had in the world, and the ONLY one he's got now; and then I happened to look around and see that paper.

It was a close place. I took it up, and held it in my hand. I was trembling, because I'd got to decide, forever, **betwixt** two things, and I knew it. I studied a minute, sort of holding my breath, and then says to myself:

"All right, then, I'll GO to hell"-- and tore it up.

It was awful thoughts and awful words, but they was said. And I let them stay said; and never thought no more about **reforming**. I **shoved** the whole thing out of my head, and said I would take up wickedness again, which was in my line, being brung up to it, and the other wasn't. And for a starter I would go to work and steal Jim out of slavery again; and if I could think up anything worse, I would do that, too; because as long as I was in, and in for good, I might as well go the whole hog.

我，总是想尽一切方法为我着想，他对我一向都这么好。最后我又想起了救他的那件事：我对人们说我们木筏子上有害天花的人，当时他是特别感谢我，说我是老杰姆在这个世上最好的朋友，也是他如今唯一的朋友。正是那时，我朝四周张望的时候碰巧看到了那张纸。

纸条离得挺近，我把它捡了起来，拿在手里。我在发抖，因为知道我得在两条路中做出选择，选择了就永远也不能反悔了。我略微屏着呼吸仔细考虑了一分钟，随后我对自个儿说：

"好吧，下地狱就下地狱吧。"我随手把纸条撕了。

这是可怕的念头，可怕的词语，不过我已经这么说了。既然话已经说出我就从没有想过要收回。我把整件事从脑袋里清理了出去。我说，我要重拾邪恶，邪恶是我的本行，我就是在邪恶的环境下长大的，走另一条路就不在行了。首先要做的第一件事儿，就是把杰姆救出奴隶的境地。如果我能想出什么更为邪恶的办法的话，我也会照干不误。因为既然我决定干这一行，那么只要有利，我就要干到底。

单词解析 Word Analysis

swamp [swɒmp] *n.* 沼泽（地）；湿地

例 The swamp teems with mosquitoes.
这片沼泽地蚊子多极了。

feud [fju:d] *n.* 不和，世仇

例 Because of a family feud she could not marry him.
由于家庭之间的宿怨她不能和他结婚。

betwixt [bɪ'twɪkst] *prep.* （古）在其间；在……中间

例 It is a strange sympathy betwixt soul and body.
这是灵魂和肉体之间一种奇妙的共鸣。

reform [rɪ'fɔ:m] *v.* 改革；改进；改良

例 The law needs to be reformed.
法律需要进行改革。

shove [ʃʌv] *v.* 推，猛推

例 The crowd was pushing and shoving to get a better view.
人们挤来挤去，想看得清楚点儿。

语法知识点 Grammar Points

① **But I didn't do it straight off, but laid the paper down and set there thinking— thinking how good it was all this happened so, and how near I come to being lost and going to hell.**

句中的两个how都引导宾语从句，作thinking的宾语。
"straight off" 立即，马上

例 She asked him straight off what he thought about it all.
她率直地问他对这一切有什么想法。

② **I'd see him standing my watch on top of his, instead of calling me, so I could go on sleeping**

"on top of" 接着

我的名著美文：人不是生来就要被打败的

例 Gale winds came on top of the floods.
大风紧接着洪水袭来。

I'd是I would的缩写，表示一种主观意愿，instead of 而不是……，两个短语放在一起，可以译为：宁愿……也不……。

③ I shoved the whole thing out of my head, and said I would take up wickedness again, which was in my line, being brung up to it, and the other wasn't.

"which"引导非限制性定语从句，指代wickedness。
"in one's line"擅长……

例 Wild guesses aren't much in my line.
瞎猜并不是我的专长。

"wasn't"代表was not

⑤ ...and if I could think up anything worse, I would do that, too; because as long as I was in, and in for good, I might as well go the whole hog.

"think up"想出，设计出，发明出

例 Can't you think up a better excuse than that?
难道你就想不出一个比这更好的借口？

"might as well"不妨

例 If no one else wants it, we might as well give it to him.
如果没人要这个，我们不妨给他吧。

"go the whole hog"彻底地做某事；干到底；尽力而为

例 If we start it, we shall go the whole hog.
要是着手干的话，我们就干到底。

经典名句 Famous Classics

1. The best mirror is an old friend.
老朋友是一面最好的镜子。

2. The best of all governments is that which teaches us to govern ourselves.
最好的政府是教导我们管理自己。

3. The best of friends must part.
   好友终有分手时。

4. Doing everything is doing nothing.
   贪多嚼不烂。

5. Doing nothing is doing ill.
   不干事就是干坏事。

6. Don't be vain because you are good looking.
   不可以美貌自骄。

7. The best of us can make mistakes.
   再杰出的人也会出错。（智者千虑，必有一失。）

8. One who never made a mistake, never made anything.
   不犯错误的人必然一事无成。

读书笔记

32 The Adventures of Tom Sawyer
汤姆·索亚历险记

They sprang away, stumbling over roots and among vines in the dark, no two plunging in the same direction. A furious blast roared through the trees, making everything sing as it went. One blinding flash after another came, and peal on peal of deafening thunder. And now a **drenching** rain poured down and the rising hurricane drove it in sheets along the ground. The boys cried out to each other, but the roaring wind and the booming thunder-blasts drowned their voices utterly. However, one by one they **straggled** in at last and took shelter under the tent, cold, scared, and streaming with water; but to have company in misery seemed something to be grateful for. They could not talk, the old sail flapped so furiously, even if the other noises would have allowed them. The tempest rose higher and higher, and presently the sail tore loose from its fastenings and went winging away on the blast. The boys seized each others' hands and fled, with many tumblings and bruises, to the shelter of a great oak that stood upon the river-bank. Now the battle was at its highest. Under

他们撒腿就跑，在黑暗中不时绊到树根和葡萄藤，他们猛冲向不同的方向。一阵猛烈的风在树丛中咆哮，所到之处都在簌簌作响。炫目的闪电一个接一个，震耳的雷声一下接着一下。现在，瓢泼大雨倾泻而下，越来越猛烈的飓风沿着地面把它们分成雨幕。男孩们互相叫嚷着，但咆哮的狂风和轰轰隆隆的雷声彻底淹没了他们的声音。不过，孩子们终于一个接一个地回到了露营地，在帐篷下躲了起来，他们又冷又怕，身上全是雨水。在这样恶劣的条件下，幸好大家守在一起。即便在其他噪音下他们能够听见彼此的声音，但是大雨拍打旧帆篷的声音太大了，他们不能听到彼此的说话声。风暴越来越猛烈，不久就把帆篷的连接点吹松动了，帆篷也飘向了大风中。男孩们紧抓住了彼此的双手逃向岸边的一棵大橡树下避雨，这一路上摔了好几跤擦破了好几个地方。这时，狂风骤雨、电闪雷鸣狂暴至极。无休止的闪电把天空照

the ceaseless **conflagration** of lightning that flamed in the skies, everything below stood out in clean-cut and shadowless distinctness: the bending trees, the **billowy** river, white with foam, the driving spray of spume-flakes, the dim outlines of the high **bluffs** on the other side, glimpsed through the drifting cloud-rack and the slanting veil of rain. Every little while some giant tree yielded the fight and fell crashing through the younger growth; and the **unflagging** thunderpeals came now in ear-splitting explosive bursts, keen and sharp, and unspeakably appalling. The storm culminated in one matchless effort that seemed likely to tear the island to pieces, burn it up, drown it to the tree-tops, blow it away, and deafen every creature in it, all at one and the same moment. It was a wild night for homeless young heads to be out in.

亮了，万物都轮廓清晰、分外鲜明：被吹弯曲的树木、白浪翻涌的大河、成片随风飞舞的泡沫，还有河对岸高耸的悬崖那朦胧的轮廓都在漂流的浮云和倾斜的雨幕中若隐若现。每隔一段时间，就有一棵大树不敌狂风，哐当一声倒在小树丛中。雷声不断、震耳欲聋、惊魂夺魄、难以形容。风暴最终的威力达到了极点，似乎要把这个岛屿撕成碎片，烧成灰烬，将它淹没到树梢，再把它吹得无影无踪，同时还要震聋岛上的所有生物。对这几个无家可归的年轻人来说，这一夜真是挺疯狂的。

单词解析 Word Analysis

drench [drentʃ] v 使湿透

- 例 A heavy shower drenched the campers.
  一阵暴雨把露营者都淋湿了。

straggle ['stræɡl] v 蔓延；散漫

- 例 Weeds straggle over the garden.
  花园里野草蔓延。

我的名著美文：人不是生来就要被打败的

conflagration [ˌkɒnfləˈgreɪʃn] *n.* 大火（灾）

例 The light of that conflagration will fade away.
这熊熊烈火会渐渐熄灭。

billowy [ˈbɪləʊɪ] *adj.* 巨浪似的，汹涌的

例 The billowy crowd bubbled again.
汹涌的人群再一次沸腾了。

bluff [blʌf] *n.* 悬崖；峭壁

例 One of the choppers set down on the beach below them, the other on the bluff above.
有一架直升机在他们下面的海滩上降落，其余的直接降落在断崖上。

unflagging [ˌʌnˈflægɪŋ] *adj.* 不倦的，持续的，不松懈的

例 He was sustained by the unflagging support of his family.
他得到了家人不断的支持。

语法知识点 Grammar Points

① **And now a drenching rain poured down and the rising hurricane drove it in sheets along the ground.**

"in sheets" 大片大片地

例 The snow came down in sheets.
大雪大片大片地落到地上。

② **Under the ceaseless conflagration of lightning that flamed in the skies, everything below stood out in clean-cut and shadowless distinctness.**

"Under the ceaseless conflagration of lightning that flamed in the skies" 作状语，其中that引导限制性定语从句，代替lightning；句子的主语为everything below。

"stand out" 突出，杰出

例 Orange flags stand out brightly, set against the blue sky.
橘黄色的旗在蓝天的映衬下显得分外鲜艳。

③ **The storm culminated in one matchless effort that seemed likely to tear the island to pieces, burn it up, drown it to the tree-tops, blow it away, and deafen every creature in it, all at one and the same moment. It was a wild night for homeless young heads to be out in.**

"culminate in/with"（以某种结果）告终，结束

例 All his efforts culminate in success.
他的所有努力以成功结束。

此外，本句涉及提喻的修辞手法（Synecdoche），homeless young heads实际上指代的是homeless young boys。

例 an useless mouth 没用的人；光吃饭不干活的人

例 Two heads are better than one. 人多力量大。

经典名句 *Famous Classics*

1. One wrong [false] move can lose the whole game.
   棋错一着，全盘皆输。

2. One wrong thought may cause a lifelong regret.
   一念之错可铸终生之恨。

3. Open not your door when the devil knocks.
   不要受人的诱惑。

4. Pouring oil on the tire is no way to quench it.
   加油不是灭火法。

5. A brave retreat is a brave exploit.
   勇退即勇进。

6. Prepare for a rain day.
   未雨绸缪。

7. Never try to prove what nobody doubts.
   无须证实那些无人怀疑的事情。

我的名著美文：人不是生来就要被打败的

8. Repetition is the mother of knowledge.
复习是学习之源。

9. Reading makes a full man, meditation a profound man, discourse a clear man.
博览群书使人完美，冥思苦想让人深邃，论证阐述使人头脑清晰。

读书笔记

33 The Call of Nature
野性的呼唤

All that stirring of old instincts which at stated periods drives men out from the sounding cities to forest and plain to kill things by chemically **propelled** leaden pellets, the bloodlust, the joy to kill--all this was Buck's, only it was infinitely more intimate. He was ranging at the head of the pack, running the wild thing down, the living meat, to kill with his own teeth and wash his muzzle to the eyes in warm blood.

There is an **ecstasy** that marks the summit of life, and beyond which life cannot rise. And such is the **paradox** of living, this ecstasy comes when one is most alive, and it comes as a complete forgetfulness that one is alive. This ecstasy, this forgetfulness of living, comes to the artist, caught up and out of himself in a sheet of flame; it comes to the soldier, war-mad on a stricken field and refusing quarter; and it came to Buck, leading the pack, sounding the old wolf-cry, **straining** after the food that was alive and that fled swiftly before him through the moonlight. He was sounding the deeps of his nature, and of the parts of his nature that were

布克体内隐藏着一种原始的本能，这个本能在特定的时期牵引人类走出城市来到森林和平原大开杀戒。现在，这种原始本能——对血的渴望、对杀戮的迷恋都属于布克。这种快感不断驱使着布克跑在狼群的前端，渴望用自己的牙齿击杀那新鲜的猎物，让自己从嘴到眼睛都浸在温热的鲜血里。

狂喜标志着生命的顶峰，而生命无法超越它。这就是一种生活的悖论，只有当一个人最活跃的时候，这种极端的状态就会出现，而它会使人浑然忘却生命的存在。这种巅峰的状态、这种超脱生命的状态，使艺术家创作的激情如烈火般爆发；使士兵成为好战分子，在战场上疯狂战斗，对敌人毫不留情；使布克带领着狼群，发出一种古老的嚎叫声，紧紧追捕那只在月光下疯狂逃窜的鲜活的食物。他的嚎叫发自内心深处，发自更深奥的本性，仿佛回溯到了时间的起点。他被时间的冲击所征服，是那种生命的轮换，是身体每块肌肉

deeper than he, going back into the womb of Time. He was mastered by the sheer surging of life, the tidal wave of being, the perfect joy of each separate muscle, joint, and sinew in that it was everything that was not death, that it was aglow and **rampant**, expressing itself in movement, flying exultantly under the stars and over the face of dead matter that did not move.

与肌腱带来的快感，因为这些让你知道自己没有死去，知道生命的活跃和狂躁，在悸动中表现自己，在群星中狂乱飞舞，飞过那些寂静不动的事物。

单词解析 Word Analysis

propel [prəˈpel] v. 推进；推动

例 He succeeded in propelling the ball across the line.
他成功地把球带过线。

ecstasy [ˈekstəsi] n. 狂喜；出神

例 One wondered what heights of ecstasy the winner reached.
人们想知道胜者欣喜若狂到了什么程度。

paradox [ˈpærədɒks] n. 自相矛盾的人或事

例 He was a paradox—a loner who loved to chat to strangers.
他这个人还真是矛盾——生性孤僻却又喜欢和陌生人闲聊。

strain [streɪn] v. 尽力；竭力；使劲

例 I strained my ears to catch what they were saying.
我竖起耳朵去听他们在说些什么。

rampant [ˈræmpənt] adj. 蔓延的；猖獗的

例 Unemployment is now rampant in most of Europe.
在欧洲的大部分地区，失业问题难以控制。

The Call of Nature
野性的呼唤

语法知识点 *Grammar Points*

① **All that stirring of old instincts which at stated periods drives men out from the sounding cities to forest and plain to kill things by chemically propelled leaden pellets, the bloodlust, the joy to kill--all this was Buck's, only it was infinitely more intimate.**

"which"引导限制性定语从句，指代"instincts"。句子的主语为三个平行结构：All that stirring、the bloodlust 和the joy to kill。

"at stated periods"在特定时期

例 Generally magazines come out at stated periods.
一般来说，杂志定时出版。

② **There is an ecstasy that marks the summit of life, and beyond which life cannot rise.**

此句话为两个小句子，连词"and"连接。"that"引导限制性定语从句，代替"ecstasy"，"which"引导非限制性定语从句，代替"the summit of life"。

③ **He was mastered by the sheer surging of life, the tidal wave of being, the perfect joy of each separate muscle, joint, and sinew in that it was everything that was not death, that it was aglow and rampant, expressing itself in movement, flying exultantly under the stars and over the face of dead matter that did not move.**

"in that"在这里充当连词，可以译为"因为"。

例 There were some holes in that theory, some unanswered questions.
那个理论中有一些漏洞，一些问题没有解答。

我的名著美文：人不是生来就要被打败的

经典名句 Famous Classics

1. The best place to find a helping hand is at the end of your own arm.
   最好的帮助应是自己的双手。（求人不如求己。）

2. Don't judge by appearance.
   不可以貌取人。

3. Don't praise the day until evening.
   一日未尽，莫赞天晴。

4. The best smell is bread, the best savour salt, the best love that of children.
   面包的气味最香，食盐的滋味最鲜，儿童的情爱最甜。

5. Don't quarrel with your bread and butter.
   不要自砸饭碗。

6. The blind man's wife needs no painting.
   瞎子的老婆不需化妆。

7. One tree does not make a forest.
   独木不成林。

8. Praise the sea, but keep on land.
   赞美着大海，却待在陆地。（叶公好龙。）

9. Poison is poison though it comes in a golden cup.
   纵然装入金杯，毒药还是毒药。

读书笔记

34 The Catcher in the Rye
麦田里的守望者

"Among other things, you'll find that you're not the first person who was ever confused and frightened and even sickened by human behavior. You're by no means alone on that score; you'll be excited and stimulated to know. Many, many men have been just as troubled morally and spiritually as you are right now. Happily, some of them kept records of their troubles. You'll learn from them—if you want to. Just as some day, if you have something to offer, someone will learn something from you. It's a beautiful **reciprocal** arrangement. And it isn't education. It's history. It's poetry."He stopped and took a big drink out of his highball. Then he started again. Boy, he was really hot. I was glad I didn't try to stop him or anything. "I'm not trying to tell you that only educated and **scholarly** men are able to contribute something valuable to the world. It's not so. But I do say that educated and scholarly men, if there brilliant and creative to begin with—which, unfortunately, is rarely the case—tend to leave infinitely more valuable records behind them than men

"接触到了很多事之后，你就会发现，你不是第一个对人类的行为感到困惑、害怕甚至是厌恶的人。在这方面，你绝对不是第一人。了解这一点会使你激动，备受鼓舞。许许多多的人正如现在的你一样，在道德和精神上都感到困惑。幸运的是，其中的一些会记录自己的烦恼。如果你愿意的话，将向他们学习。正如某一天，如果你有了可以教授别人的东西，就会有人向你学习，这是非常美妙又互惠互利的安排。而且，这不是教育，这是历史，这是诗。"他说到这儿停了下来，喝了一大口冰水饮料，接着他又继续往下说。哦，他说得正在兴头上，我很庆幸自己没有做打断他之类的事情。他说："我不是想和你说，只有受过教育、有学识的人才能对世界作出贡献。但我的确承认受过教育、有学识的人，如果一开始他们也是既聪明又极具创造力（但实际上这种情况很少），相比于仅仅是才华横溢又具有创造精

do who are merely brilliant and creative. They tend to express themselves more clearly, and they usually **have a passion for** following their thoughts through to the end. And—most important—nine times out of then they have more **humility** than the unscholarly thinker. Do you follow me at all?"

"Yes, sir."

He didn't say anything again for quite a while. I don't know if you've ever done it, but it's sort of hard to sit around waiting for somebody to say something when they're thinking and all. It really is. I kept trying not to yawn. It wasn't that I was bored or anything—I wasn't—but I was so damn sleepy all of a sudden.

"Something else an academic education will do for you. If you go along with it any considerable distance, it'll begin to give you an idea what size mind you have. What it'll fit and, maybe, what it won't. After a while, you'll have an idea what kind of thoughts your particular size mind should be wearing. For one thing, it may save you an extraordinary amount of time trying on ideas that don't suit you, aren't becoming to you. You'll begin to know your true measurements and dress your mind accordingly."

神的人，他们可能会留下更多宝贵的记录。他们往往能更加清晰地表达自己的想法，也喜欢从始至终坚持自己的想法。而且——最重要的是——他们十个中有九个比那些没学识的思考者更谦虚。你明白我的意思吗？"

"我明白，先生。"

他有好一会儿没再吭声。我不知道你是否有过这经历，不过坐在那里等别人说话，眼看着他一直在思索着，实在很不好受。的确很不好受。我尽力不让自己打呵欠。倒不是我觉得无聊——真的不是——可我突然困得要命。

"学校教育还能给你带来别的好处。你受的教育到了一定程度，就会发现自己的头脑有多大的能耐。它适合什么，以及或许不适合什么。过了一段时期，你就会知道你这样的头脑应当有什么样的思想。主要是，这样可以为你节省大量的时间，免得你去尝试一些不合适、不贴切的事情。你将渐渐了解自己的头脑并恰如其分地把它包装起来。"

The Catcher in the Rye
麦田里的守望者 **34**

单词解析 Word Analysis

reciprocal [rɪ'sɪprəkl] *adj.* 相互的；互惠的

例 The two colleges have a reciprocal arrangement whereby students from one college can attend classes at the other.
两所学院有一项互惠协定，允许学生在院际间选课。

scholarly ['skɒləli] *adj.* 学术性的

例 Faculty members devote most of their time to scholarly research.
全院教师大部分时间都用来从事学术研究。

have a passion for 非常喜欢……

例 I have a passion for both Chinese and basketball.
我对汉语和篮球都很热衷。

humility [hjuː'mɪləti] *n.* 谦逊，谦恭

例 Their daughter's death had taught him humility.
他们女儿的死使他学会了谦逊。

语法知识点 Grammar Points

① **Many, many men have been just as troubled morally and spiritually as you are right now.**

此句运用了比较特殊的"as...as"结构的定语从句。第一个as为副词，后者为关系代词作从句的宾语。

② **If you go along with it any considerable distance, it'll begin to give you an idea what size mind you have.**

"what size mind you have"作give的直接宾语，也为"an idea"的补语。

例 I can give what you want.
你想要的一切我都可以给你。（what you want作give的直接宾语）

③ **For one thing, it may save you an extraordinary amount of time trying on ideas that don't suit you, aren't becoming to you.**

"for one thing" 首先；一方面

例 For one thing, he didn't trust his legs to hold him up.
主要是，他不相信自己能站起来。

"becoming"在本句中相当于fitting或suitable，为"合适的"之意。

例 It was not very becoming behaviour for a teacher.
这种举止与一个教师的身份不太相称。

经典名句 *Famous Classics*

1. A door must be either shut or open.
   非此即彼。

2. Money is round, and rolls away.
   财富无常。

3. People who live in glass houses should not throw stones.
   自己有缺点，莫挑别人短。

4. Trust not before you try.
   未调查，莫相信。

5. No answer is also an answer.
   沉默也是一种回答。

6. Truth and oil are ever above.
   真相如同油，总会浮出水面。

7. Adversity leads to prosperity.
   逆境通向成功。

8. All roads lead to Rome.
   条条大路通罗马。

9. One never loses by doing a good turn.
   行善者决无一失。

35 The French Lieutenant's Women
法国中尉的女人

She turned to look at him—or as it seemed to Charles, through him. It was not so much what was positively in that face which remained with him after that first meeting, but all that was not as he had expected; for theirs was an age when the favored feminine look was the **demure**, the obedient, the shy. Charles felt immediately as if he had **trespassed**; as if the Cobb belonged to that face, and not to the Ancient Borough of Lyme. It was not a pretty face, like Ernestina's. It was certainly not a beautiful face, by any period's standard or taste. But it was an unforgettable face, and a tragic face. Its sorrow welled out of it as purely, naturally and unstoppably as water out of a woodland spring. There was no **artifice** there, no **hypocrisy**, no **hysteria**, no mask; and above all, no sign of madness. The madness was in the empty sea, the empty horizon, the lack of reason for such sorrow; as if the spring was natural in itself; but unnatural in welling from a desert.

Again and again, afterwards, Charles thought of that look as a lance; and to think so is of course not merely

他转过身看向他，不过，在查尔斯看来，她仿佛看穿了他。初次邂逅后，令查尔斯难以忘怀的不是她脸上表现出来的东西，而是她表现出的神色与他的预料不同。他们生活的年代，受欢迎的女性形象是端庄娴静、顺从心意、娇羞可爱的。查尔斯立刻感到，似乎整条科布堤并不属于古老的莱姆镇，而是属于这张脸，而他就像是一个闯进了她的领地的外来者。她不像欧内斯蒂娜那样美丽，就任何时期的审美标准来说，她的脸都谈不上是一张美丽的面庞。不过，这是一张令人难以忘怀的面容，一张面带愁容的面容。她的脸上流露出的尽是忧伤，就像泉水从林中喷泉涌现一样，既自然又无休无止。她的脸上没有诡计，没有虚情假意，没有歇斯底里，也没有伪善的面具；最重要的是，没有丝毫神经错乱的痕迹。这种忧伤，只属于苍茫的大海和空旷的地平线。自作多情的悲伤，就好像喷泉，其本身很自然，但从沙漠中出现就很不寻常。

157

to describe an object but the effect it has. He felt himself in that brief instant an unjust enemy; both **pierced** and deservedly diminished.

The woman said nothing. Her look back lasted two or three seconds at most; then she resumed her stare to the south. Ernestina **plucked** Charles's sleeve, and he turned away, with a shrug and a smile at her. When they were nearer land he said, "I wish you hadn't told me the sordid facts. That's the trouble with provincial life. Everyone knows everyone and there is no mystery. No romance."

She teased him then: the scientist, the despiser of novels.

一次又一次地，查尔斯把那副神情视为矛；当然了，不是描述那神情本身，而是指它具有的影响。他在那短短的一瞬间觉着自己是一个可憎的敌人，仿佛被一眼看穿，活该被消减。

那位女士缄默不语。她回头看了一眼，最多也就停留了两三秒钟，随后她继续望向南边。欧内斯蒂娜扯了一下查尔斯的衣袖，查尔斯转过身朝着她耸了一下肩，摆出一个微笑。当他们走远些，查尔斯说："我倒真希望你没有告诉我那肮脏的现实。乡下生活就这点不好：人们对彼此的一切都了如指掌，没有神秘感，也没有浪漫情调。"

欧内斯蒂娜取笑查尔斯：只知道科学，却不懂什么轶事趣闻。

单词解析 Word Analysis

demure [dɪˈmjʊə(r)] *adj.* 娴静的；谦恭的；庄重的
- She's very demure and sweet.
  她非常娴静可爱。

trespass [ˈtrespəs] *v.* <律>侵占，侵入；侵犯
- He told me I was trespassing on private land.
  他说我在擅闯私人领地。

artifice [ˈɑːtɪfɪs] *n.* 灵巧；诡计
- His remorse is just an artifice to gain sympathy.
  他的悔恨只是一种骗局，是为了博取同情。

The French Lieutenant's Women 法国中尉的女人

hypocrisy [hɪ'pɒkrəsi] *n.* 伪善，虚伪

例 They left themselves wide open to accusations of double standards and hypocrisy.
他们使自己陷于被人指责搞双重标准和虚伪不实的境地。

hysteria [hɪ'stɪəriə] *n.* （特指女人的）歇斯底里

例 There's a very thin dividing line between joviality and hysteria.
激动和歇斯底里之间就一线之隔。

pierce [pɪəs] *v.* 刺穿，戳穿；刺破

例 Make sure that you do not pierce the skin when boning the chicken thighs.
剔鸡腿骨时切勿戳破外面的皮。

pluck [plʌk] *v.* 拉，拽

例 He plucked the baby out of her arms.
他从她怀里夺过宝宝。

语法知识点 Grammar Points

① **It was not so much what was positively in that face which remained with him after that first meeting, but all that was not as he had expected.**

"It is/was not..., but..." 不是……而是……

例 But it was not your fault but mine.
不是你的错，而是我的错。

"not so much...as..." 与其说……不如说……

例 He is not so much a journalist as a writer.
与其说他是个新闻工作者，不如说他是个作家。

② **There was no artifice there, no hypocrisy, no hysteria, no mask; and above all, no sign of madness.**

"above all" 在这里的意思为：最重要的是。

159

例 Above all, keep in touch.
最要紧的是保持联系。

③ Her look back lasted two or three seconds at most; then she resumed her stare to the south.

"at most" 至多；最多；充其量

例 As a news item it merits a short paragraph at most.
作为一则新闻，它至多只能占一小段。

"resume to do" 继续做……

例 The gymnasium is being upholstered, and it will resume to open in one month.
健身房正在装修中，一个月后恢复正常营业。

经典名句 Famous Classics

1. The best swimmers are oftenest drowned.
   善游者溺。

2. The end makes all equal.
   死亡面前，人人平等。

3. Nothing endures but truth.
   真理永存。

4. The best teacher one can have is necessity.
   我们能得到的最好老师是"需要"。

5. The best wine comes out of an old vessel.
   酒是越陈越好。

6. No smoke without some fire.
   无风不起浪。

7. Not possession, but use, is the only riches.
   拥有却不用并非财富。

8. Nothing but is good for something.
   凡事皆有用处。（天生我材必有用。）

The French Lieutenant's Women 法国中尉的女人

9. The better the day, the better the deed.
日子越美好,事业越顺当。

读书笔记

36 The Gift of the Magi
麦琪的礼物

For there lay The Combs—the set of combs, side and back, that Della had worshipped long in a Broadway window. Beautiful combs, pure tortoise shell, with jewelled rims—just the shade to wear in the beautiful **vanished** hair. They were expensive combs, she knew, and her heart had simply **craved** and yearned over them without the least hope of possession. And now, they were hers, but the tresses that should have adorned the **coveted** adornments were gone.

But she hugged them to her bosom, and at length she was able to look up with dim eyes and a smile and say: "My hair grows so fast, Jim!"

And then Della leaped up like a little singed cat and cried, "Oh, oh!"

Jim had not yet seen his beautiful present. She held it out to him eagerly upon her open palm. The dull precious metal seemed to flash with a reflection of her bright and **ardent** spirit.

"Isn't it a dandy, Jim? I hunted all over town to find it. You'll have to look at the time a hundred times a day now. Give me your watch. I want to see how

原来（包裹里的东西）是一套梳子——全套梳子，包括梳两鬓的，梳后面的，样样俱全。这套梳子是德拉很久之前在百老汇的橱窗里见过的，自此她就非常喜欢这套梳子。这些美丽的发梳，是纯玳瑁做的，边上镶着珠宝——其色彩正好同她失去的秀发相配。只是她知道这套梳子很贵，她一点儿都不敢奢求自己可以拥有这套梳子。现在，这套梳子属于她了，但是她却不再拥有美丽的长发来衬托这垂涎已久的装饰品。

不过，她依然把发梳抱在胸前，过了好一阵子才抬起含泪的双眸，微笑着说："我的头发长得很快的，吉姆！"

随后，德拉活像一只因被烫伤而跳起来的小猫，欢快地叫着："对了，对了！"

吉姆还没有瞧见他的美丽的礼物呢。她迫不及待地把手掌摊开，递到他面前。那暗色的贵重金属闪着光，似乎反射着她开朗又热忱的心情。

"它漂亮吗，吉姆？我搜

it looks on it."

Instead of obeying, Jim tumbled down on the couch and put his hands under the back of his head and smiled.

"Dell," said he, "let's put our Christmas presents away and keep 'em a while. They're too nice to use just at present. I sold the watch to get the money to buy your combs. And now suppose you put the chops on."

遍了全城才找到了它。现在,你会每天看一百次时间的。把表给我,我要看看它配在表上怎么样。"

吉姆没有拿出表,反而倒在沙发上,两手撑着后脑勺,脸上还挂着微笑。

"亲爱的,"他说,"让我们先把各自的圣诞礼物收起来保存一阵子吧。现在它们还派不上用场。我把我的金表卖了,换回了你的梳子。现在去准备排骨吧。"

单词解析 Word Analysis

vanish ['vænɪʃ] *v.* 消失;突然不见;消亡,消灭

例 He just vanished and was never seen again.
他就这么消失了,再也没人见到过他。

crave [kreɪv] *v.* 恳求,请求;渴望

例 She has always craved excitement.
她总渴望刺激。

covet ['kʌvət] *v.* 贪求,觊觎

例 He had long coveted the chance to work with a famous musician.
他一直渴望有机会与著名音乐家一起工作。

ardent ['ɑːdnt] *adj.* 热情的

例 Some ardent supporters were urging him to stand.
一些热心支持者正在力劝他参选。

语法知识点 Grammar Points

① **They were expensive combs, she knew, and her heart had simply craved and yearned over them without the least hope of possession.**

"without the least hope of possession" 作状语，可译为：不带有丝毫可以拥有它们的奢望。

② **But she hugged them to her bosom, and at length she was able to look up with dim eyes and a smile and say: "My hair grows so fast, Jim!"**

此句涉及了一语双叙的修辞手法（Syllepsis）。"with dim eyes and a smile"，此短语是由一个介词引导的两个名词的结构，且每个名词都可以被此介词修饰。

例 He went to school in a hurry and a taxi.
他乘出租车急匆匆地赶去了学校。
Yesterday he had blue heart and coat.
昨天，穿着蓝色大衣的他很伤心。

③ **The dull precious metal seemed to flash with a reflection of her bright and ardent spirit.**

"with a reflection of" 反射出，反射着……

例 In fact, this drama has a strong political color, and is closely related to the current events with a reflection of the times.
实际上，这部剧有很强的政治色彩，也能反映时事。

经典名句 Famous Classics

1. The Bible and a stone do well together.
   圣经与石头交替使用。（要恩威并用，软硬兼施。）

2. Nothing worse than a familiar enemy.
   知我者最危险。

3. Of all wars, peace is the end.
   一切战争终将以和平告终。

4. Poverty breeds strife.
   贫穷引起冲突。

5. Poverty makes a man mean.
   贫穷使人小气。

6. Once a devil, always a devil.
   一次做魔鬼，永远是魔鬼。

7. Poverty is a pain, but no disgrace.
   贫困虽痛苦，但并非是耻辱。

8. Poverty is no shame, laziness is.
   贫穷不可耻，懒惰才可耻。

9. A clean conscience fears not false accusations.
   身正不怕影子斜。

读书笔记

37 The Grapes of Wrath
愤怒的葡萄

The western, nervous under the beginning change. The Western States, nervous as horses before a thunder storm. The great owners, nervous, sensing a change, knowing nothing of the nature of the change. The great owners, striking at the immediate thing, the widening government, the growing labor unity; striking at new taxes, at plans; not knowing these things are results, not causes. Results, not causes; results, not causes. The causes lie deep and simple—the causes are a hunger in a stomach, **multiplied** a million times; a hunger in a single soul, hunger for joy and some security, multiplied a million times; muscles and mind aching to grow, to work, to create, multiplied a million times. The last clear definite function of man—muscles aching to work, minds aching to create beyond the single need—this is man. To build a wall, to build a house, a dam, and in the wall and house and dam to put something of Manself, and to Manself take back something of the wall, the house, the dam; to take hard muscles from the lifting, to take the clear lines and form

变动刚刚开始,西部地区就紧张了起来。西部各州犹如风暴前夕的马一样惊恐慌乱。大业主们觉察到了变化,但由于他们对这个变化的本质一无所知,他们紧张了起来。大业主们遇到了种种紧迫的问题,他们不知道这些问题是结果而非起因;他们试图应付日益扩大的政府控制和日益增大的劳动集团,他们试着应付新的税收政策以制定出新计划。这些问题是结果,而不是起因。是结果,并非起因。起因的根源很深,却很简单——起因是胃中的饥饿,这种饥饿被放大了一百万倍;是每个人心灵对快乐和些许安全感的渴望,这种渴望被放大了一百万倍;是身体和精神对发展、工作和创造的渴求,这种渴求被放大了一百万倍。人类最明确的一个特征是急于工作的身体和急于创造不只满足个人需求的思想,这就是人。修建一堵墙、一座房子、一个大坝,再把人的精神放到这堵墙、这座房子、这个大坝里面,反过来人类又

from **conceiving**. For man, unlike any other thing **organic** or inorganic in the universe, grows beyond his work, walks up the stairs of his concepts, emerges ahead of his accomplishments. This you may say of man—when theories change and crash, when schools, philosophies, when narrow dark alleys of thought, national, religious, economic, grow and disintegrate, man reaches, stumbles forward, painfully, mistakenly sometimes. Having stepped forward, he may slip back, but only half a step, never the full step back. This you may say and know it and know it. This you may know when the bombs **plummet** out of the black planes on the market place, when prisoners are stuck like pigs, when the crushed bodies drain **filthily** in the dust. You may know it in this way. If the step were not being taken, if the **stumbling**-forward ache were not alive, the bombs would not fall, the throats would not be cut. Fear the time when the bombs stop falling while the bombers live—for every bomb is proof that the spirit has not died. And fear the time when the strikes stop while the great owners live—for every little beaten strike is proof that the step is being taken. And this you can know—fear the time when Manself will not suffer and die for a concept, for this one

从这堵墙、这座房子、这个大坝里面得到些什么——从举重中得到坚实的肌肉，从思考中获取清晰的轮廓和形式。人类不同于宇宙中任何其他的有机体或无机体，他们要在自身工作范围外获得发展，顺着自己的观念的阶梯向上前行并在自己的成就前崭露头角。你可以这样说人类——当各种理论改变或者崩塌的时候，当各个学派、哲学，当民族、宗教、经济方面的思想道路由于狭隘又阴暗而破碎的时候，人类有时会朝着错误的方向前进，痛苦地跌倒。人类向前迈了一步，之后人类可能会后退，但绝不会退一整步，他们只会退半步。你不妨这样说或是了解一下这个（比喻）。当炸弹从黑色飞机投往市集时，当囚犯们像猪一样被刺穿身体，当不再完整的身体在被血液染红的尘土中流干时，你也许就知道了这个道理。如果人不跨出那一步，如果跌倒了也前进的渴望不再强烈，炸弹就不会落下了，喉咙也不会被刺穿了。当炸弹停止投掷而投炸机还存在着，这是令人害怕的——因为每一个炸弹都代表了不灭的精神。当罢工停止了而大业主们还存在着，这是令人害怕的——因为每次罢

167

quality is the foundation of Manself, and this one quality is man, distinctive in the universe.

工都证明了前进的步伐。还有你可以明白的：当人类不愿意为了一种概念受罪甚至是牺牲时，这是令人害怕的——因为这种品质是人类自身的基石，这也是人类区别于宇宙中其他万物的品质。

单词解析 Word Analysis

multiply ['mʌltɪplaɪ] *v.* （使）相乘；（使）增加

例 Our problems have multiplied since last year.
自去年以来，我们的问题成倍增加。

conceive [kən'siːv] *v.* 构思；想象，设想

例 God is often conceived of as male.
上帝常常被想象为男性。

organic [ɔː'gænɪk] *adj.* 有机（体）的；有组织的

例 Today, organic wine producer is typically a small, quality-conscious family concern.
如今，有机葡萄酒生产商一般是注重品质的小型家族企业。

plummet ['plʌmɪt] *v.* 垂直落下；骤然跌落

例 The jet plummeted into a row of houses.
那架喷气式飞机一头栽进一排房子里。

filthy ['fɪlθi] *adj.* 污秽的，不洁的

例 He never washed, and always wore a filthy old jacket.
他总是穿着一件从来不洗的脏兮兮的旧夹克。

stumble ['stʌmbl] *v.* 跌跌撞撞地走，蹒跚；失足

例 We were stumbling around in the dark looking for a candle.
黑暗中，我们东跌西撞地找蜡烛。

语法知识点 *Grammar Points*

① **The Western States, nervous as horses before a thunder storm.**

此句涉及明喻（Simile）的修辞手法，把西部各州比作风暴来临前的马。

例 If one has anything to say, it drops from him simply and directly as a stone falls to the ground.
如果一个人有什么想说的，从他嘴中说出的话语就会像石子落到地上一样简单直接。

② **The causes lie deep and simple—the causes are a hunger in a stomach, multiplied a million times; a hunger in a single soul, hunger for joy and some security, multiplied a million times; muscles and mind aching to grow, to work, to create, multiplied a million times.**

句中的三个"multiplied"是非谓语动词，表示被动，其形式主语分别是a hunger in a stomach，a hunger in a single soul, hunger for joy and some security和muscles and mind aching to grow, to work, to create。

本句运用了夸张（Hyperbole）的修辞手法，以突出要强调的部分。

例 She wept oceans of tears.
她泪如汪洋。（用夸张的手法来强调她流了很多眼泪）

The old man lived a year in a minute without his grandson.
没有孙子的陪伴，这个老人度日如年。（运用夸张的手法来体现老人对孙子的依恋）

Thanks a million. 万分感谢。
（夸张的手法来表达自己非常感谢对方）

③ **To build a wall, to build a house, a dam, and in the wall and house and dam to put something of Manself, and to Manself take back something of the wall, the house, the dam; to take hard muscles from the lifting, to take the clear lines and form from conceiving.**

"Manself"一词运用了仿拟（Parody）的修辞手法，由myself, yourself, herself, himself等推演出了Manself（人类自己）。
如：由air pollution（空气污染），water pollution（水污染）推演出了noise pollution（噪声污染）。

由generation gap（年龄差），production gap（生产差距）推演出了knowledge gap（知识差距）。

> ④ Fear the time when the bombs stop falling while the bombers live—for every bomb is proof that the spirit has not died. And fear the time when the strikes stop while the great owners live—for every little beaten strike is proof that the step is being taken.

"Fear the time"是祈使句结构，省略了主语you。
when引导时间状语从句，for引导原因状语从句。在语义和情感上这两句话是层层递进的，先是从一个简明易懂的例子出发，再引出目前社会存在的问题。

经典名句 Famous Classics

1. Out of frying pan into the fire.
   刚出龙潭，又入虎穴。

2. One can't please everybody.
   众口难调。

3. A clay idol fording a river is hardly able to save itself.
   泥菩萨过河，自身难保。

4. Poverty is the reward of idleness.
   贫困是对懒惰的惩罚。

5. Never say of another what you would not have him hear.
   莫说不想让人听见的话。

6. Never show the bottom of your purse or your mind.
   钱包不露底，思想需保留。

7. A child may have too much of his mother's blessing.
   妈妈对孩子过于溺爱，反而会惯坏孩子。

8. Never think yourself above your business.
   切勿眼高手低。

9. Never too late to mend.
亡羊补牢，犹未为晚。

读书笔记

38 The Great Gatsby
了不起的盖茨比

He looked around him wildly, as if the past were **lurking** here in the shadow of his house, just out of reach of his hand.

"I'm going to fix everything just the way it was before,"he said, nodding determinedly. "She'll see."

He talked a lot about the past, and I gathered that he wanted to recover something, some idea of himself perhaps, that had gone into loving Daisy. His life had been confused and disordered since then, but if he could once return to a certain starting place and go over it all slowly, he could find out what that thing was...

One autumn night, five years before, they had been walking down the street when the leaves were falling, and they came to a place where there were no trees and the sidewalk was white with moonlight. They stopped here and turned toward each other. Now it was a cool night with that mysterious excitement in it which comes at the two changes of the year. The quiet lights in the houses were humming out into the darkness and there was a stir and bustle

他发疯似的望向四周，仿佛过去就潜伏在房子的暗处，只是他够不到而已。

"我会把一切安排得同过去一样，"他一边说着一边还点着头，似乎心意已决，"她会明白的。"

关于过去，他谈了很多，我估计他是想要恢复点儿什么东西，也许是他关于自己的一些想法，这些想法都融化在对黛西的爱意中了。自从迷上黛西后，他的生活就开始变得混乱不堪，但如果他能够回到起点，一切都慢慢来的话，他就能发现那东西是什么了……

五年前一个深夜，正是落叶纷飞的时候，他们沿街散步，走到了一处没有树木的人行道，整个街道都笼罩在白色的月光下。他们停在了那里，面对面地站着。那正是两季交替时期的一个夜晚，十分凉爽，空气中充满了这一时期特有的神秘感和激奋感。房屋里的灯光静静地洒进黑暗里；星星在闪烁着、舞动着。盖茨比用余光看到一排排人行道真的变成了一个梯

among the stars. Out of the corner of his eye Gatsby saw that the blocks of the sidewalks really formed a ladder and mounted to a secret place above the trees—he could climb to it, if he climbed alone, and once there he could suck on the pap of life, **gulp** down the incomparable milk of wonder.

His heart beat faster and faster as Daisy's white face came up to his own. He knew that when he kissed this girl, and forever wed his **unutterable** visions to her perishable breath, his mind would never **romp** again like the mind of God. So he waited, listening for a moment longer to the tuning-fork that had been struck upon a star. Then he kissed her. At his lips' touch she blossomed for him like a flower and the **incarnation** was complete.

子，它穿过树林通向一个神秘的地方——只要是他一个人攀登，他就能够攀到那个神秘的地方，一旦上到那儿他便可以吮吸生命的乳汁，尽情饮下那能创造出奇迹的甜美琼浆。

当黛西白皙的脸庞离他越来越近时，他的心跳得越来越快。他知道如果他吻了这个姑娘，将他无法表达的憧憬和她随时可能消失的呼吸永远锁结在一起的话，他的心将不再像上帝之心那般可以自由驰骋、随心所欲。于是，他等待着，多听了一会儿音叉敲在星辰上传来的声音。然后，他吻了她。在触碰到她的芳唇的一刹那，黛西像一朵娇嫩的花苞为他绽放了，于是这个理想的化身就完成了。

单词解析 Word Analysis

lurk [lɜːk] v 潜伏，埋伏

例 Why are you lurking around outside my house?
你在我房子外面鬼鬼祟祟的，想干什么？

gulp [gʌlp] v 狼吞虎咽地吃，吞咽

例 He gulped down the rest of his tea and went out.
他把剩下的茶一饮而尽便出去了。

unutterable [ʌnˈʌtərəbl] adj. 说不出的；难以形容的

例 I am at the beginning of a new and unutterable loneliness.
我再次陷入莫名的孤独寂寞中。

我的名著美文：人不是生来就要被打败的

romp [rɒmp] v. 欢快地迅速奔跑
例 Dogs and little children romped happily in the garden.
狗和小孩子们在花园里嬉戏。

incarnation [ˌɪnkɑːˈneɪʃn] n. 化身；前身；典型体现
例 She is a perfect incarnation of glamour.
她是魅力的完美化身。

语法知识点 Grammar Points

① **He looked around him wildly, as if the past were lurking here in the shadow of his house, just out of reach of his hand.**

"in the shadow of" 在……的影子下（庇佑下）；在……附近
例 He felt safe in the shadow of the Lord God.
他在上帝的庇护下感到安全。

"out of reach of" ……够不到，对……来说遥不可及
例 Keep breakables out of reach of very young children.
把易碎物品放在小孩子够不到的地方。

② **Now it was a cool night with that mysterious excitement in it which comes at the two changes of the year.**

"with that mysterious excitement in it" 为状语，it指代night。
"which" 引导限制性定语从句，代指it，即night。
"come at" 袭击；威胁；找到；得到
例 Economically and politically, this affair couldn't come at a worse time.
无论从经济上还是政治上来看，这件事来得都太不是时候了。

③ **At his lips' touch she blossomed for him like a flower and the incarnation was complete.**

"at +n." 可译为"当……时"
例 At this news, she cried for a whole day.
听到了这个消息，她哭了一整天。
此句采用明喻（Simile）的修辞手法，"like a flower"像花一样。

speak like a book 咬文嚼字
stand like a log 呆若木鸡

例 They are like peas and carrots.
他们形影不离。

经典名句 *Famous Classics*

1. No entertainment is so cheap as reading nor any pleasure so lasting.
   没有比读书更便宜的娱乐，也没有比读书更持久的快乐。

2. None but the brave deserves the fair.
   英雄方可配美人。

3. A clean mouth and an honest hand will take a man through any land.
   礼貌待人，事事顺利。

4. A clear conscience is a soft pillow.
   问心无愧，高枕无忧。

5. No extreme will hold long.
   物极必反。

6. No fence against (an) ill fortune.
   篱笆挡不住厄运。（厄运难逃。）

7. A close mouth catches no flies.
   口风紧，不招祸。

8. No fool like an old fool.
   老年荒唐无药可救。

9. No gains without pains.
   不劳则无获。

39 The Lord of the Flies
蝇王

A little boy who wore the remains of an extraordinary black cap on his red hair and who carried the remains of a pair of **spectacles** at his waist, started forward, then changed his mind and stood still.

"We saw your smoke. And you don't know how many of you there are?"

"No, sir."

"I should have thought," said the officer as he **visualized** the search before him, "I should have thought that a pack of British boys—you're all British, aren't you?—would have been able to put up a better show than that—I mean—"

"It was like that at first," said Ralph, "before things—"

He stopped.

"We were together then—"

The officer nodded helpfully.

"I know. Jolly good show. Like the Coral Island."

Ralph looked at him dumbly. For a moment he had a **fleeting** picture of the strange glamour that had once invested the beaches. But the island was **scorched** up like dead wood—Simon

一个红头发的小男孩向前走了过来,他头戴一顶款式特别的黑色帽子,只不过它已经破烂不堪了;腰上别着一副破碎的眼镜。走着走着他改变了想法,停在那儿不动了。

"我们看到你们的烟雾了。可你们不知道你们共有多少人?"

"是的,先生。"

"我本该想到,"军官想象着之前的搜查,说道:"我应该想到一群英国男孩——你们是英国男孩吧?——在一块应该比刚刚玩得更好,我是说——"

"一开始,我们玩得很好,"拉尔夫说,"但后来——"

他停了一下。

"那时,我们还在一起——"

军官点点头,鼓励拉尔夫继续说下去。

"我知道了。像珊瑚岛一样精彩的表演。"

拉尔夫木讷地望着他。一瞬间,拉尔夫的脑海里飞速划过曾带给海滩一种神奇魅

was dead—and Jack had.... The tears began to flow and sobs shook him. He gave himself up to them now for the first time on the island; great, **shuddering spasms** of grief that seemed to **wrench** his whole body. His voice rose under the black smoke before the burning wreckage of the island; and infected by that emotion, the other little boys began to shake and sob too. And in the middle of them, with filthy body, matted hair, and unwiped nose, Ralph wept for the end of innocence, the darkness of man's heart, and the fall through the air of the true, wise friend called Piggy.

The officer, surrounded by these noises, was moved and a little embarrassed. He turned away to give them time to pull themselves together; and waited, allowing his eyes to rest on the trim cruiser in the distance.

力的画面。但是这座小岛已经被烧得像枯木一样——西蒙死了——杰克已经……杰尔夫的眼泪滚落下来，由于哭泣身体一颤一颤地抖着。他放任自己尽情哭泣，这是他上岛以来第一次这样做。一阵阵由悲伤引起的抽搐似乎把他身体扭成一团。他面前残余的岛屿继续燃烧着，浓烟升起，他的哭泣响彻整个岛屿。受这种情绪的影响，其他男孩子们也都啜泣起来。拉尔夫站在孩子们中间，肮脏不堪、蓬头垢面，甚至连鼻子都没有来得及擦拭，他为童真的泯灭和人性的黑暗哭泣，也为他忠实又聪明的朋友"猪崽子"的倒下而哭泣。

军官被环绕的哭泣声打动了，有一点不知所措。他转过身，给他们点儿时间让他们平复一下心情；他盯着远处整洁的巡航舰，稍作休息。

单词解析 Word Analysis

spectacle ['spektəkl] *n.* 眼镜

例 I need to buy new spectacle frames but I will keep the old lenses.
我需要买新的眼镜框，不过我会留着旧镜片。

visualize ['vɪʒuəlaɪz] *v.* 形成思维图像；设想

例 He could not visualize her as old.
他想象不出她年老时的样子。

我的名著美文：人不是生来就要被打败的

fleeting ['fliːtɪŋ] *adj.* 疾驰的，飞逝的；短暂的

例 The world is like a fleeting show.
人世如白驹过隙。

scorch [skɔːtʃ] *v.* 烧焦，烤焦

例 Don't stand so near the fire—your coat is scorching!
别站得离火那么近——你的外衣都快烤焦了！

shuddering ['ʃʌdərɪŋ] *adj.* 令人战栗的

例 She drew a deep shuddering breath.
她不由得打了个寒噤，深深吸了口气。

spasm ['spæzəm] *n.* 痉挛；抽搐

例 A spasm of pain brought his thoughts back to the present.
一阵剧痛把他的思绪拉回到了现在。

wrench [rentʃ] *v.* 扭伤；扭转；歪曲

例 She wrenched her knee when she fell.
她跌倒时把膝盖扭伤了。

语法知识点 *Grammar Points*

① I should have thought that a pack of British boys—you're all British, aren't you?—would have been able to put up a better show than that—I mean—

"a pack of" 一堆；一群

例 It shows a fox being disembowelled by a pack of hounds.
画面中一只狐狸正被一群猎狗撕咬得肠子外流。

"put up a better show" 上演一场更好的演出

例 His Ferrari team will be hoping to put up a better show this Sunday.
他的法拉利车队希望会在这周日有一个出色的表现。

② And in the middle of them, with filthy body, matted hair, and unwiped nose, Ralph wept for the end of innocence, the darkness of man's heart, and the fall through the air of the true, wise friend called Piggy.

"weep for" 为……而哭泣

例 When you live next to the cemetery, you cannot weep for everyone.
如果你住公墓附近，你不能为每一个逝者哀悼。

③ He turned away to give them time to pull themselves together; and waited, allowing his eyes to rest on the trim cruiser in the distance.

"turn away" 转过脸去

例 Walking straight up, he was upon him before he could turn away.
他一直走上前去，不等对方转身走开，就招呼起来。

"pull oneself together" 振作起来；定神

例 It was only by a supreme effort of will and courage that he was able to pull himself together.
他全凭超凡的决心和勇气才使自己振作起来。

经典名句 Famous Classics

1. A cold hand and a warm heart.
   刀子嘴，豆腐心。

2. Practice is the best master.
   实践出真知。

3. A disease should be treated early; an evil should be rooted out.
   治病要趁早，除害要除了。

4. Push generally succeeds in business.
   在事业上埋头苦干通常就会成功。

179

5. A few are no match for the many.
   寡不敌众。

6. Punctuality is the politeness of kings.
   守时乃国王之礼。（守时非常重要。）

7. Put the cart before the horse.
   本末倒置。

8. A dog that will bemired tries to bemire others.
   沾上污泥的狗尽力要把污泥弄到别的狗身上。

9. Put the saddle on the right horse.
   惩罚分明。

读书笔记

40 The Merchant of Venice
威尼斯商人

人物简介：

鲍西娅（Portia）：富家女，机智勇敢，巴萨尼奥之妻。为救丈夫的朋友女扮男装作为法庭的顾问。

安东尼奥（Antonio）：资产阶级商人，珍视友情，为了朋友向高利贷者借钱并为此死而无怨。

巴萨尼奥（Bassanio）：安东尼奥的朋友，曾向安东尼奥借钱。

葛莱西安诺（Gratiano）：巴萨尼奥的侍从，他疾恶如仇，易于激动，嬉笑怒骂，敢于斗争。

Portia: You, merchant, have you any thing to say?

Antonio: But little. I am armed and well-prepared. Give me your hand, Bassanio, and fare you well! **Grieve** not that I am fallen to this for you. Commend me to your honorable wife: Say how I loved you, speak me fair in death; And, when the tale is told, bid her be judge whether Bassanio had not once a love.

Bassanio: Antonio, I am married to a wife which is a dear to me as life itself, but life itself, my wife, and all the world are not with me esteemed above thy life. I would sacrifice them to this devil for you.

鲍西娅：商人，你还有什么话说吗？

安东尼奥：我没什么要说的了，我已经准备好了。把你的手给我，巴萨尼奥，永别了！不要因为我是为了你才落得如此下场而悲伤。替我向尊夫人致意，告诉她我有多么爱你，告诉她我是怎样从容就死；等到你讲完这些，请她判断一句，巴萨尼奥是不是曾经有一个真心爱他的朋友。

巴萨尼奥：安东尼奥，我视我的妻子如我的生命；可是我的生命、我的妻子以及整个的世界，在我的眼中都不比你的生命更为珍贵；我愿意失去

181

Portia: Your wife would give you little thanks for that, if she were by, to hear you make the offer.

Shylock: We waste time. Come.

Portia: **Tarry** a little. This bond **doth** give thee here no jot of blood; the words expressly are "a pound of flesh". Take, then, **thy** bond. But, in the cutting it, if thou dose shed one drop of Christian blood, thy lands and goods are by the laws of Venice **confiscate** unto Venice.

Bassanio: Oh, upright judge! Mark, Jew; A Daniel has come to judgement!

Shylock: Is that the law?

Portia: As **thou** urgest justice, thou shalt have justice, more than thou desirest.

Shylock: I take this offer, then. Pay the bond thrice and let the Christian go.

Bassanio: Here is the money.

Portia: Soft. The Jew shall have all justice. Soft; no haste. He shall have nothing but the penalty.

Gratiano: A second Daniel! A Daniel, Jew!

Portia: Why doth the Jew pause? Take thy forfeiture.

Shylock: Give me my principal, and let me go.

Portia: He hath refused it in the open court. He shall have merely justice and his bond.

这一切,牺牲它们给这恶魔,来救出你的生命。

鲍西娅:尊夫人要是就在这儿,听见您说这样的话,恐怕不见得会感谢您吧。

夏洛克:别再浪费时间了,快点儿宣判吧。

鲍西娅:且慢。这约上他的一滴血也不允许你取,只是写着"一磅肉",所以你可以照约拿一磅肉去。不过在割肉的时候,要是淌下一滴基督徒的血,按照威尼斯的法律,你的土地和其他所有物就要全部充公。

巴萨尼奥:啊,公平正直的法官!听着,犹太人,博学多才又睿智的法官啊,简直是但以理再世!

夏洛克:法律是这样规定的吗?

鲍西娅:既然你要求公道,我就给你公道,而且比你所求还公道。

夏洛克:那么我愿意接受还款。照约上的数目的三倍还我,就放了那基督徒。

巴萨尼奥:钱在这儿。

鲍西娅:别急。这位犹太人必须得到绝对的公道。别急,慢慢来。他只能照约处罚(安东尼奥),不能接受其他的赔偿。

葛莱西安诺:这简直是但

Bassanio: A Daniel, still I say; A second Daniel! I thank thee, Jew, for teaching me that word.

Shylock: Shall I not have barely my principal?

Portia: Thou shall have nothing but thy **forfeiture**, to be taken at thy peril.

Shylock: Why, then the devil give him good of it!

Portia: Tarry, Jew. The law hath yet another hold on you. By the laws of Venice, your wealth is **forfeited** to the state for having **conspired** against the life of one of its citizens. Your life lies at the mercy of him you conspired against. Therefore, down on your knees, and beg pardon.

以理转世啊！一个公平正义又睿智的法官，是个犹太人！

鲍西娅：那犹太人为什么还不动手？没收你的财产。

夏洛克：把我的本钱还我，放我走吧。

鲍西娅：他已经当庭拒绝过了。我们现在只能给他公道，让他履行原约。

巴萨尼奥：好一个但尼尔，再世的但以理！谢谢你，犹太人，你教会我说这句话。

夏洛克：难道我单单拿回我的本钱都不成吗？

鲍西娅：犹太人，你只能冒着你自己的财产被充公的危险，你不能拿一分钱。

夏洛克：好，那么魔鬼保佑他去享用吧！我不打这场官司了。

鲍西娅：等一等，犹太人，法律上还有一点牵涉你。威尼斯的法律规定：凡是企图谋害任何一位威尼斯公民者，他的财产要没入公库，犯罪者的生命悉听受害人处置，他人不得过问。证据表明，你已经违反了此项法规，快快跪下来，请求原谅吧。

单词解析 *Word Analysis*

grieve [gri:v] v. （使）伤心；（使）悲伤
- 例 She grieved the death of her husband.
  她为丈夫的去世而悲伤。

tarry ['tæri] v. 逗留；停留
- 例 Two old boys tarried on the street corner discussing cattle.
  两个大男孩在街角停留许久，一直在讨论牛。

doth [dʌθ] v. （古）do的第三人称单数现在式
- 例 Doth this bring thee no comfort?
  这一点难道还不能给你带来慰藉吗？

thy [ðaɪ] pron. （古）你的（相当于your）
- 例 Love thy neighbour as thyself.
  爱邻如爱己。

confiscate ['kɒnfɪskeɪt] v. 没收；充公
- 例 Their land was confiscated after the war.
  他们的土地在战后被没收。

thou [ðaʊ] pron. （古）你（相当于you）
- 例 Thou nor I have made the world.
  创造这个世界的既不是你也不是我。

forfeiture ['fɔːfɪtʃə(r)] n. （财产等的）没收，（权利、名誉等的）丧失
- 例 Forfeiture of bills is an unusual situation in the circulating of bills.
  票据丧失是票据流转中的异常情况，而且票据丧失还经常与票据伪造相联系。

forfeit ['fɔːfɪt] v. （因违反协议、犯规、受罚等）丧失，失去
- 例 If you cancel your flight, you will forfeit your deposit.
  乘客取消航班订位，定金概不退还。

conspire [kən'spaɪə(r)] v. 搞阴谋；协力促成
- 例 They were accused of conspiring against the king.
  他们被指控阴谋反对国王。

语法知识点 Grammar Points

① **Grieve not that I am fallen to this for you.**

祈使句的否定形式，动词放在句首，然后再接否定词not，相当于"Don't grieve that I am fallen to this for you."其中that引导宾语从句。

② **Say how I loved you, speak me fair in death; And, when the tale is told, bid her be judge whether Bassanio had not once a love.**

"Say how I loved you, speak me fair in death"为祈使句，用动词原形。
"fair in death"译为"从容就死"。
"a love"在这里指一个朋友，即为安东尼奥自己。

③ **I am married to a wife which is a dear to me as life itself, but life itself, my wife, and all the world are not with me esteemed above thy life. I would sacrifice them to this devil for you.**

"as"是"像……一样的意思"，"but"关系连词，表转折，连接两句话。"above"在……之上，超过。"for"用介词来表示动作，暗含"来换取"的意思。

④ **A Daniel has come to judgement!**

此句话运用了隐喻（metaphor）的修辞手法。Daniel这个名字的含义是"God is my judge"，含有公平正义之意。因此此句要表达的是像但以理一样既公正又睿智。

例 Money is the lens in a camera.
　　钱很重要。（镜头对相机来说是很重要的，而钱就像是镜片一样，暗含也是很重要的）
　　the nose of a ship 船头
　　the eye of a flower 花蕊
　　the lip of the cup 杯口

经典名句 Famous Classics

1. A clear mouth stream is avoided by fish.
　　水至清则无鱼。

我的名著美文：人不是生来就要被打败的

2. Of illness comes no goodness.
   一懒生百邪。

3. Old habits die hard.
   陈规陋习难消除。

4. A fox cannot hide its tail.
   狐狸尾巴藏不住。

5. Quick returns make rich merchant.
   周转一快，就能致富。

6. A friend in need is a friend indeed.
   患难见真情。

7. Rain before seven; fine before eleven.
   早雨不过午。

8. A dog has his day.
   凡人皆有得意之日。

9. Rats desert a falling house.
   房子倒，老鼠跑。

读书笔记

41 The Plain Man and His Wife
平凡人和他的妻子

The plain man on a plain day wakes up, slowly or quickly according to his temperament, and greets the day in a mental **posture** which might be thus expressed in words: "Oh, Lord! Another day! What a grind!"

If you ask me whom I mean by the plain man, my reply is that I mean almost every man. I mean you. I certainly mean me. I mean the rich and the poor, the successful and the unsuccessful, the idle and the diligent, the luxurious and the **austere**. For, what with the limits of digestion, the practical impossibility of wearing two neckties at once, the insecurity of investments, the responsibilities of wealth and success, the exhaustingness of the search for pleasure, and the cheapness of travel—the real differences between one sort of plain man and another are slight in these times. (And indeed they always were slight.)

……

Oh! But he chose his vocation. He likes it. It satisfies his instincts. It is his life. (So you say.) Well, does he like it? Does it satisfy his instincts? Is it his

平凡人在平凡的一天醒来，他动作的快慢取决于他那天的心情如何。他迎接这一天的内心想法要是用文字来表述就是："天哪！又是一天！太遭罪了！"

如果你问我这个平凡人指谁，我的回答是：每个人，包括你，当然也包括我；包括穷人，也包括富人；包括成功人士，也包括非成功人士；包括懒散的人，也包括勤奋的人；包括奢侈的人，也包括节俭的人。由于每个人的消化能力有限，同时佩戴两条领带不现实；投资有风险；成功和富有意味着责任；寻乐终究会精疲力竭；旅行很廉价——现如今，一种平凡人与另一种平凡人的实际差距很小。（其实，一直以来都挺小的。）

……

哦！但职业是他自己选的，他喜欢。职业可以满足他的本能，是他的生活（你可以这么说）。那么，他喜欢这份职业吗？这份职业真的能满足他的本能吗？即便答案是肯

life? If truly the answer is affirmative, he is at any rate not conscious of the fact. He is aware of no ecstasy. What is the use of being happy unless he knows he is happy? Some men know that they are happy in the hours of business, but they are few. The majority are not, and the bulk of the majority do not even pretend to be. The whole attitude of the average plain man to business implies that business is a nuisance, scarcely mitigated. With what secret satisfaction he anticipates that visit to the barber's in the middle of the morning! With what **gusto** he hails the arrival of an unexpected interrupting friend! With what easement he decides that he may lawfully put off some task till the morrow! Let him hear a band or fire-engine in the street, and he will go to the window with the eagerness of a child or of a girl-clerk. If he were working at golf, the bands of all the **regiments** of Hohenzollern would not make him turn his head, nor the **multitudinous** blazing of fireproof **skyscrapers**. No! Let us be honest. Business constitutes the steepest, roughest league of the appointed path. Were it otherwise, business would not be universally regarded as a means to an end.

定的，平凡人自己还没有意识到。他没有感受到喜悦。如果感受不到喜悦，那么快乐又有什么用处呢？有些人知道自己在工作时是快乐的，但这类人很少。大部分人还是不知道，这部分人的绝大部分连假装快乐都不会。一般来说，平凡人对工作的整体态度表明工作很烦人，一直很烦人！他心中期待上午十点左右去理发店，别提这份心情有多满足了！有打断他工作的不速之客时，别提他有多高兴了！他将一些工作合理地推迟到第二天，别提他有多么轻易了！当他听到街上有乐队或消防车的声音，他就会像小孩儿或女店员一样迫切地跑到窗边。如果他在打高尔夫，即使霍亨索伦王室整个军团都出动了，或是一大片防火大楼都在燃烧，他也连头都不会转一下的。不，说实话吧。工作是必经之路上最陡峭、最艰难的一段。不然的话，大家不会普遍认为工作是达成目标的一种手段。

单词解析 Word Analysis

posture [ˈpɒstʃə(r)] *n.* 看法；态度；姿势

例 The government has adopted an aggressive posture on immigration.
政府对移民入境采取了强硬的态度。

austere [ɒˈstɪə(r)] *adj.* 朴素的，简朴的

例 The room was austere, nearly barren of furniture or decoration.
房间非常简朴，几乎没有任何家具和装饰。

gusto [ˈɡʌstəʊ] *n.* 热情，乐趣

例 They sang with gusto.
他们兴致勃勃地唱歌。

regiment [ˈredʒɪmənt] *n.* （军队的）团；大量的人或物

例 The regiment secured its position while awaiting the enemy attack.
该团在等待敌人进攻之时加强了防御工事。

multitudinous [ˌmʌltɪˈtjuːdɪnəs] *adj.* 大量的，群集的，多种多样的

例 I heard again the multitudinous murmur of the city.
我又听到了城市里各种各样的嗡嗡声。

skyscraper [ˈskaɪskreɪpə(r)] *n.* 摩天大楼，超高层大楼

例 The skyscraper stands 500 feet.
摩天大楼高达500尺。

语法知识点 Grammar Points

① **If truly the answer is affirmative, he is at any rate not conscious of the fact.**

"if" 在此句中是 "即使，即便" 之意。

例 We'll only do it once — if at all.
我们就是干也只会干一次。

"at any rate" 无论如何，至少

例 I may be away on business next week but at any rate I'll be back by Friday.
我下周可能要出差，但无论如何，我最晚星期五回来。

② **With what secret satisfaction he anticipates that visit to the barber's in the middle of the morning! With what gusto he hails the arrival of an unexpected interrupting friend! With what easement he decides that he may lawfully put off some task till the morrow!**

"with..."引导的三个句子为平行结构。且每个句子都为感叹句。本句中的感叹句结构为"what（+adj.）+ n.（不可数名词）"。

例 What delicious food it is!
这个食物多么美味呀！

③ **Were it otherwise, business would not be universally regarded as a means to an end.**

此句涉及虚拟条件句的用法，当if引导的从句中有"should、had、were"时，要把这三个词提前至句首，并省略if。

例 Were I in your position, I would go.
如果我是你的话，我就会走。（其完整句子应为：If I were in your position, I would go.）

经典名句 *Famous Classics*

1. A dog is made fat in two meals.
   狗吃两顿就肥。（三年清知府，十万雪花银。）

2. One must howl with the wolves.
   入乡随俗。

3. Money is the key that opens all doors.
   金钱是打开一切门户之钥匙。

4. One never loses anything by politeness.
   礼多不吃亏。（礼多人不怪。）

The Plain Man and His Wife
平凡人和他的妻子

5. Money is something, but not everything.
   金钱能买到一些东西，但不是万能的。

6. A full belly counsels well.
   衣食足而后知荣辱。

7. Money is the root of (all) evil.
   金钱是万恶之源。

8. Ninety percent of inspiration is perspiration.
   灵感是汗水浇灌出来的。

9. News is like fish.
   新闻就像鱼，过后不新鲜。

读书笔记

42 The Rainbow
彩虹

So the Brangwens came and went without fear of necessity, working hard because of the life that was in them, not for want of the money. Neither were they **thriftless**. They were aware of the last halfpenny, and instinct made them not waste the peeling of their apple, for it would help to feed the cattle. But heaven and earth was **teeming** around them, and how should this cease? They felt the rush of the **sap** in spring, they knew the wave which cannot halt, but every year throws forward the seed to **begetting**, and, falling back, leaves the young-born on the earth. They knew the intercourse between heaven and earth, sunshine drawn into the breast and **bowels**, the rain sucked up in the daytime, nakedness that comes under the wind in autumn, showing the birds' nests no longer worth hiding. Their life and interrelations were such; feeling the pulse and body of the soil, that opened to their furrow for the grain, and became smooth and **supple** after their ploughing, and clung to their feet with a weight that pulled like desire, lying hard and unresponsive when the crops

所以，布朗温一家没有生活之忧。他们辛勤劳作，是天性使然，并非因为缺钱。他们注意不把钱花光，他们本能地不扔掉苹果皮，因为苹果皮可以用来喂牛。他们周围，天地生生不息，怎么会休止呢？春天，他们能感受到活力的涌现，其浪潮永无休止，每年都抛撒出生命的种子，种子再落回大地，土地上再长出新生命。他们了解天地的阴阳交汇——阳光照进大地的五脏六腑，大地又在白昼吸入雨露，在秋风中赤裸无余，鸟儿再无藏身之处。他们的生活和相互关系就是如此：感受着土地的脉搏，土地在开垦后满是种庄稼用的犁沟，土壤变得又松又软，一踩上去，它像欲望一样紧紧抓住你。而到了快要收割庄稼时，土地就变得坚实硬朗了。一株株稚嫩的谷物像海浪一样随风起伏，像腿边的绸缎般丝滑光洁。他们捧起奶牛的乳房挤奶，奶牛一边产奶一边抵抗人们的手掌，奶头的血脉冲撞着人们手中的命脉。他们跨上马背，双腿夹紧生命。他们把马套

were to be shorn away. The young corn waved and was silken, and the **lustre** slid along the limbs of the men who saw it. They took the **udder** of the cows, the cows yielded milk and pulse against the hands of the men, the pulse of the blood of the teats of the cows beat into the pulse of the hands of the men. They mounted their horses, and held life between the **grip** of their knees, they harnessed their horses at the wagon, and, with hand on the bridle-rings, drew the heaving of the horses after their will.

到马车前，手握缰绳，随心所欲地勒住暴躁的马儿。

单词解析 Word Analysis

thriftless ['θrɪftlɪs] *adj.* 浪费的

例 Thus, he has terrible fits of remorse and repentance; but he is lavish and thriftless all the same.
因此，他一阵阵地非常自责、悔恨；但是他还是那样铺张浪费。

teem [tiːm] *v.* 充满，富于

例 Fish teem in this stream.
这条小河里鱼很多。

sap [sæp] *n.* 精力；活力

例 The world's whole sap is sunk.
整个世界元气大伤。

beget [bɪ'get] *v.* 产生，引起

例 Economic tensions beget political ones.
经济紧张导致政治紧张。

我的名著美文：人不是生来就要被打败的

bowel ['baʊəl] *n.* 肠；内部
例 A rumble came from the bowels of the earth.
从地下深处传来隆隆的响声。

supple ['sʌpl] *adj.* （身体）柔软的；灵活的
例 These exercises will help to keep you supple.
这些锻炼项目有助于你保持身体的柔韧性。

lustre ['lʌstə(r)] *n.* 光泽；光荣
例 Her hair had lost its lustre.
她的头发失去了光泽。

udder ['ʌdə(r)] *n.* （牛、羊等的）乳房
例 The calf fumbled for its mother's udder for milk.
小牛摸索着妈妈的乳房找奶吃。

grip [grɪp] *n.* 紧握，抓牢
例 She struggled from his grip.
他紧拉住她不放，她奋力挣脱。

语法知识点 Grammar Points

① So the Brangwens came and went without fear of necessity, working hard because of the life that was in them, not for want of the money.

"fear of" 对……恐惧
例 Ignorance of people brings fear, fear of the unknown.
人们的无知会带来恐惧，对未知事物的恐惧。

"for want of" 缺少
例 The plants died for want of water.
这些植物因缺水而枯死了。

② They were aware of the last halfpenny, and instinct made them not waste the peeling of their apple, for it would help to feed the cattle.

"for" 引导原因状语从句，"it" 指代 "the peeling of their apple"。

"be aware of" 知道；意识到

例 He doesn't seem to be aware of the problems.
　　他好像没有意识到这个问题。

③ **Their life and interrelations were such; feeling the pulse and body of the soil, that opened to their furrow for the grain, and became smooth and supple after their ploughing, and clung to their feet with a weight that pulled like desire, lying hard and unresponsive when the crops were to be shorn away.**

"and became smooth and supple after their ploughing" 和 "and clung to their feet with a weight that pulled like desire" 是并列句，其主语都为 "soil"，"lying hard and unresponsive when the crops were to be shorn away" 中的 lying 是非谓语动词，表示主动的动作或状态；when 引导时间状语从句。

"cling to" 坚持；紧抓

例 He appears determined to cling to power.
　　看来他决心要抓住权力不放。

经典名句 Famous Classics

1. Cards are the devil's books.
   赌博是万恶之源。

2. You can't touch pitch without being defiled.
   近朱者赤，近墨者黑。

3. One should not run with the hare and hunt with the hounds.
   切莫两面讨好。

4. Perseverance is vital to success.
   不屈不挠是成功之本。

5. You cannot clap with one hand.
   孤掌难鸣。

6. Opportunity makes the thief.
   疏忽招盗贼。

7. Praise without profit puts little in the pot.
   廉价的表扬不能当饭吃。

8. Care brings grey hair.
   忧虑催人老。

9. Penny wise and pound foolish.
   精明于一文，糊涂于一磅。（小事聪明，大事糊涂。）

读书笔记

43 The Scarlet Letter
红字

The young woman was tall, with a figure of perfect elegance on a large scale. She had dark and abundant hair, so glossy that it threw off the sunshine with a **gleam**, and a face which, besides being beautiful from regularity of feature and richness of complexion, had the impressiveness belonging to a marked brow and deep black eyes. She was ladylike, too, after the manner of the feminine gentility of those days; characterised by a certain state and dignity, rather than by the delicate, **evanescent**, and indescribable grace, which is now recognised as its indication. And never had Hester Prynne appeared more ladylike, in the antique interpretation of the term, than as she issued from the prison. Those who had before known her, and had expected to behold her dimmed and **obscured** by a disastrous cloud, were astonished, and even startled, to perceive how her beauty shone out, and made a halo of the misfortune and **ignominy** in which she was enveloped. It may be true, that, to a sensitive observer, there was something **exquisitely** painful in it. Her attire,

那个年轻的妇女身材修长，体态优美至极。她的秀发乌黑又浓密，在阳光下熠熠生辉；她五官端正，面色有光泽；她双眉鲜明，双瞳漆黑。按照当时女性举止优雅的风范来看，她也当属一位淑女；不过她是端庄的形象，而不是如今人们心中的那种纤弱、易逝、无法描述的优雅。即便从就当时对淑女的理解而言，海斯特·白兰从狱中走出的时刻是最像个淑女的。那些之前就认识她的人以为她在经历这场暴风似的灾难后会黯然失色，但此刻他们震惊了，甚至惊呆了，因为他们发现她容光焕发，在她所遭受的不幸和耻辱外环绕着一圈光环。不过，目光敏锐者可能会从中观察到极度的痛苦。她的衣服是她在狱中为了这个特别的时刻而准备的，其设计凭借她自己的想象，其特有的不羁和别致像是在传达她精神境界和无所顾忌的心情。但吸引了所有人目光的是她胸前绣着的闪闪的红字，那红字妙不可言以至于那

197

which, indeed, she had wrought for the occasion, in prison, and had modelled much after her own fancy, seemed to express the attitude of her spirit, the desperate recklessness of her mood, by its wild and picturesque peculiarity. But the point which drew all eyes, and, as it were, transfigured the wearer—so that both men and women, who had been familiarly acquainted with Hester Prynne, were now impressed as if they beheld her for the first time—was that SCARLET LETTER, so fantastically embroidered and illuminated upon her bosom. It had the effect of a spell, taking her out of the ordinary relations with humanity, and enclosing her in a sphere by herself.

些与她熟识的男男女女像是初次见海斯特·白兰一般。这个红字有种魔力，把她从普通人际关系中脱离出来，紧紧包裹在自身的氛围中。

单词解析 Word Analysis

gleam [gli:m] v.（使）闪烁，（使）闪亮

例 There was a gleam of hope for a peaceful settlement.
还有一线和平解决的希望。

evanescent [ˌi:vəˈnesnt] adj. 迅速消失遗忘的

例 It disappeared as evanescent as snowflakes on a river.
它瞬即消失，如雪花落入河中。

obscure [əbˈskjʊə(r)] v. 使……模糊不清

例 The view was obscured by fog.
雾中景色朦胧。

ignominy [ˈɪgnəmɪni] n. 耻辱，污辱

例 They suffered the ignominy of defeat.

他们蒙受了失败的耻辱。

exquisitely [ekˈskwɪzɪtlɪ] *adv.* 强烈地；剧烈地

例 He found her exquisitely beautiful.
他觉得她异常美丽。

语法知识点 *Grammar Points*

① **She had dark and abundant hair, so glossy that it threw off the sunshine with a gleam, and a face which, besides being beautiful from regularity of feature and richness of complexion, had the impressiveness belonging to a marked brow and deep black eyes.**

句子的主干是"She had dark and abundant hair and a face"face后接了一个限制性定语从句"which had the impressiveness belonging to a marked brow and deep black eyes"，"so glossy that it threw off the sunshine with a gleam"是插入语，修饰的是头发；"besides being beautiful from regularity of feature and richness of complexion"也是插入语，修饰的是脸。

"throw off"（向空中）释放，散发出

例 The star grew 30% brighter and threw off huge amounts of radiation.
那颗星的亮度增加了30%并释放出大量辐射。

② **Those who had before known her, and had expected to behold her dimmed and obscured by a disastrous cloud, were astonished, and even startled, to perceive how her beauty shone out, and made a halo of the misfortune and ignominy in which she was enveloped.**

本句主干为"Those...were astonished, and even startled, to perceive..."，"who"引导限制性定语从句，"how"引导宾语从句。

"behold"看，注视

例 They beheld a bright star shining in the sky.
他们看到了一颗明亮的星在天空中闪闪发光。

③ **It had the effect of a spell, taking her out of the ordinary relations with humanity, and enclosing her in a sphere by herself.**

我的名著美文：人不是生来就要被打败的

句子的主干是"It had the effect of a spell"，"taking"和"enclosing"作伴随状语。

经典名句 Famous Classics

1. Other men live to eat, while I eat to live.
   别人为食而生活，我为生活而进食。

2. You cannot serve God and Mammon.
   你不能信奉上帝，又供养财神。（信神者不能贪财。）

3. You cannot spin and reel at the same time.
   你不能既纺纱又绕线。（一心不可二用。）

4. A bad compromise is better than a good lawsuit.
   吃亏的和解也比胜诉强。

5. Perseverance is failing nineteen times and succeeding the twentieth.
   失败十九次，到第二十次成功，这就叫坚持。

6. One sin opens the door for another.
   一个罪恶为另一个罪恶开门。（坏事干一次，便有第二次。）

7. A bird that loves to sing does not make a nest.
   爱叫的鸟儿不做窝。

8. One swallow does not make a spring.
   孤燕不报春。

读书笔记